Praise for
Experiential Intelligence

"*Experiential Intelligence* delivers a simple yet powerful framework for next-generation leaders to delve deeper into how their life's experiences shape who they are and how they show up and lead."
—Jennifer Sparks Taylor, Director of Corporate Relations & Executive Education, Center for Effective Organizations, USC Marshall School of Business

"*Experiential Intelligence* uses powerful storytelling to take us on a journey to deeply understand our own XQ and how to maximize the impact it has on our leadership and business success."
—Pat Verduin, PhD, Chief Technology Officer, Colgate-Palmolive

"The ability to understand your inherent capabilities as a product of life experiences is the essence of experiential intelligence. Leaders can harness XQ to unlock their own hidden strengths and that of their teams to drive transformation."
—Valencia Bembry, Vice President of Philanthropy, United Nations Foundation

"With the increased awareness of how an individual's unique contributions and lived experiences can bring about transformation to the workplace, the new lens of experiential intelligence broadens the talent conversation and opens possibilities for building a more diverse workforce."
—Rebecca Romano, Global Head of Talent & Organizational Development, NBCUniversal

"*Experiential Intelligence* is a long overdue blueprint to more intentionally access the mindsets, abilities, and know-how gained from your unique life experience. I highly recommend that you add this book to your learning journey."

—Michael J. Arena, Vice President of Talent & Development, Amazon Web Services and former Chief Talent Officer, General Motors

"Experiential intelligence complements IQ and EQ to comprehensively assess and build the disruptive capacity of your employees and organization."

—Rich Goudis, Executive Vice Chairman, Tupperware Brands and former CEO, Herbalife Nutrition

"*Experiential Intelligence* provides an approach for how to gain self-awareness into your unique assets to foster both personal and professional growth. Soren's book gives keen insights into how the experiences we have form our current mindsets and how to examine our own self-limiting beliefs."

—Kathryn J. Coleman, PhD, Senior Vice President, Talent, Learning & Insights, 3M

"*Experiential Intelligence* reveals how to create a culture of empowerment and innovation that enables true sustainable growth and engagement."

—Rachael Orleans, Head of Change & Transformation, Cigna

"Soren Kaplan wades courageously into a half century of deep and often polarizing research on human intellect and emerges with a brilliant synthesis that provides the much-needed third leg of the intelligence stool. Experiential intelligence is the perfect complement to IQ and EQ."

—Matthew E. May, coauthor of *What A Unicorn Knows: How Leading Entrepreneurs Use Lean Principles to Drive Sustainable Growth*

"Reframing who and how we hire is more important than ever! With shifting strategies, priorities, and a quickly changing world, companies should be looking at the metrics for employees that really matter. *Experiential Intelligence* is the ultimate guide to equip leaders to know who has the talent they need to propel their business into the future."

—Dr. Marshall Goldsmith. Thinkers50 #1 Executive Coach and *New York Times* bestselling author of *The Earned Life, Triggers,* and *What Got You Here Won't Get You There*

"*Experiential Intelligence* provides an enlightening look at how to achieve personal and professional success and satisfaction."

—Michael Isip, President & CEO, KQED, PBS Public Media, San Francisco

"'Learning by doing' has long been a tenet of the educational process as it motivates and promotes participation. I am grateful to finally have a book that provides concrete examples of how experiential learning can shape the mindsets, abilities, and skills that not only help students succeed, but can also lead to personal growth, development, and success for the adults who work with them!"

—Maura Palmer, Superintendent, Salem New Hampshire Public School District

"In a world in which false assumptions are regularly at play in human relations, this book mines the treasures latent in all human beings and helps us welcome unknown talent in ourselves and others."

—Kent Packard-Davis, President, Women Forward International

"Many successful performers don't have Ivy League degrees, so there are clearly indicators of readiness beyond academic credentials. So what is the comparative value of fifteen years of experience? Does experiential intelligence deliver something a prestigious college degree does not? These are important questions to consider. From an equity perspective, we also know that both race and socioeconomics can unfairly limit education and career potential. This understanding helps companies recalibrate for and reconsider individual potential, while delivering improved access to untapped talent pools."

—Melissa Jones, Executive Vice President and
Chief Human Resources Officer,
California State Automobile Association Insurance Group

"*Experiential Intelligence* artfully blends concrete research with compelling storytelling to clearly show what leads to success. Let Soren Kaplan guide you to higher performance as a leader and for your organization."

—Juan Sanchez, Group Vice President, HCA Healthcare

"This must-read book delivers deep insight into how our personal and professional experiences influence how we show up and perform at work, in our relationships, and life itself."

—Dr. Loressa Cole, CEO, American Nurses Association

EXPERIENTIAL INTELLIGENCE

Also by Soren Kaplan

The Invisible Advantage: How to Create a Culture of Innovation

Best Business Book

———

Leapfrogging: Harness the Power of Surprise
for Business Breakthroughs

Best Leadership Book

EXPERIENTIAL INTELLIGENCE

Harness the Power
of Experience for Personal
and Business Breakthroughs

SOREN KAPLAN

Matt Holt Books
An Imprint of BenBella Books, Inc.
Dallas, TX

Matt Holt is an imprint of BenBella Books, Inc.
10440 N. Central Expressway
Suite 800
Dallas, TX 75231
benbellabooks.com
Send feedback to feedback@benbellabooks.com

BenBella and *Matt Holt* are federally registered trademarks.

Printed in the United States of America
10 9 8 7 6 5 4 3 2 1

Library of Congress Control Number: 2022029768
ISBN 9781637742020 (hardcover)
ISBN 9781637742037 (electronic)

Editing by Katie Dickman
Copyediting by Lydia Choi
Proofreading by Ariel Fagiola and Marissa Wold Uhrina
Indexing by Elise Hess
Text design and composition by Jordan Koluch
Cover design by Brigid Pearson
Cover image © Shutterstock / ImHope
Printed by Lake Book Manufacturing

Contents

INTRODUCTION

W e need to leave. They're coming to get us!"

My mother jarred me out of my sleep with a two-handed shake and shuttled my little sister and me out of the house and into our faded brown two-door 1973 Datsun. Off we went into the darkness. She drove until we reached a house in a neighboring town where she parked. I didn't know where we were, but I felt relieved to see that my mother's intensity had ratcheted down, at least enough that she was no longer shaking. I was seven; I didn't have much choice but to follow my mother's directions.

We jumped out of the car, beelining for a space in the hedge the power company had cleared for access to the meter. The three of us hunkered down in this prickly little cave in someone's front yard. And waited. We sat for twenty minutes in silence.

Like a flash of lightning, headlights lit up the hedge, and another car parked behind ours.

"Is that you?"

It was my father. I immediately felt safe. But that didn't last long. Just then the door of the house opened, and a crack of light flooded into the front yard. Out came the charismatic man I recognized as the one who had influenced my parents to drop out of Harvard University and move to California to join his spiritual community. That night when my father had come home to our empty house, he'd intuited that we would be here. And we were. With an embarrassed shake of his head, my father shuttled us kids into his own car and drove us home, my mother trailing behind alone.

That poignant episode became etched into my visceral memory. It was the first time I realized that my mother's infectious fear wasn't based in reality. It wouldn't be until years later that I would understand her behavior as the result of mental illness. But at the time, all I could do was start trying to discern for myself what was real versus what were delusional stories—not an easy task for a first grader. My challenging childhood required me to navigate a series of unusual circumstances. Yet as difficult as they were, these early experiences fostered my capacity to live with uncertainty, manage ambiguity, and find meaningful patterns in complexity—abilities that have continued to serve me well.

When I was four, my rebellious behavior convinced my parents that I was possessed. For six months, they led prayer groups in our home to expel my "demon." As my mother spiraled into mental illness, her condition was originally viewed by friends and family as a "metaphysical awakening." My father, consumed by his work and spiritual community, was rarely present. As my parents struggled to make ends meet, we bounced around from one home to another. By the time I was fifteen, I had moved sixteen times.

So, what happens to someone like me? My life could have gone in any of three directions: 1) I could have been completely overcome by my circumstances, 2) I could have gone through the motions of leading a "normal" life while blindly being led by inner scars, or 3) I could have found a way to tap into my, let's say, "unique" experiences to take command of my future. For a long time, I did the second one really well. But now, I do the third with decent success.

You probably don't share the circumstances of my early life. Most people don't. But you have your own experiences. No matter how big or small, how ordinary or extraordinary, your experiences most likely impacted you in some way or another. My own relatively extreme stories influenced me in ways that I eventually needed to face head-on—and then make choices about what to do with what I found. The process of exploring the positive and negative impacts of my experiences led me to realize that most of us are in the same boat. We all have the opportunity to more deeply understand and then explicitly leverage what we've gained from our life events, whatever they may be. This book shares what I've learned over the years working on myself, and working with thousands of leaders around the world, so that you can apply the insights and tools I've discovered to yourself, with your team, and for your organization.

Growing up, I had to take charge. I assumed responsibilities at a young age that most children never take on. My early life experiences were tough, yet I gained certain things from them that I was able to draw upon later in life. Without being aware of how I did it at the time, I successfully channeled my challenging experiences into personal strengths that led to business success. I tapped into my hidden "assets" so that, before age thirty, I became the leader of a strategy team within a Fortune 500 corporation in Silicon Valley. I founded and ran several companies, including a consulting firm focused on helping managers from around the world understand how to become better leaders by embracing uncertainty, living with ambiguity, and proactively shaping the future through innovation. I obtained clients like Disney, NBCUniversal, 3M, Kimberly-Clark, Colgate-Palmolive, Philips, Cisco, Hershey's, Red Bull, PepsiCo, Lowe's, Medtronic, Ascension Health, Kaiser Permanente, The American Nurses Association, AARP, Cigna, State Farm, and many others. I worked with executives to build business strategies, innovate their products and services, and reinvent their organizational cultures. I've harnessed my own ability to navigate uncertainty by founding several startups, including my latest venture, Praxie.com, a software company focused on digitizing the expertise developed from people's professional experiences and turning it into "best-practice" tools and business processes that anyone can instantly apply to their work.

In his book *Outliers*, Malcolm Gladwell popularized the idea that doing anything for ten thousand total hours, which is about five years of doing something full-time, makes someone an expert. The ten-thousand-hour rule mostly focuses on hard skills, like practicing the violin, working in project management, or doing something technical.

In my own case, I spent about fifteen years navigating my chaotic childhood, sorting fact from fiction, and seeking patterns to make sense of confusing behavior. It's fair to say that my formal résumé began during that time because these are the same things that I've applied in my work life while leading startup teams, managing innovation, and transforming organizational cultures. They're abilities I continually draw upon, especially in my professional life. I didn't acquire them in school, but rather from lived experience.

Up until I graduated high school, I spent most of my summers with my grandfather. He was a World War II veteran, a fashion designer in New York City, and a friend of Andy Warhol, Larry Rivers, Man Ray, and many other modern artists in the 1960s, '70s, and '80s. I learned a lot early on about the nature of trauma from his volatile behavior. What seemed like random outbursts at the time I now know were connected to the PTSD he acquired from his experiences in the war. Despite his trauma, we shared many positive moments together. My grandfather taught me about the nature of creativity. He introduced me to his artist friends. He shared his love of photography with me. He showed me how to look at crumbling buildings, graffiti, and garbage on the streets and in the alleys of New York as beauty, while we took photographs together of the concrete landscape. He gave me insight into the concept of originality and how new-to-the-world ideas deliver a feeling of positive surprise when people experience them, which in turn grabs attention and inspires word-of-mouth marketing. He showed me how the value of a work of art is a combination of being the first to do something and the unique story of the artist. I learned a lot about what it takes to introduce into the world creative ideas that stick. I put my experiences with my grandfather to use as I went on to formally study innovation in graduate school and then practice it in business.

I grew up in the San Francisco Bay Area, the region in Northern California known for welcoming diverse thinking and challenging conventional norms. Within this bubble of progressive culture, my life was intertwined with my parents' alternative spiritual community. In my teenage eyes, I viewed my parents as blindly following the teachings of their guru and his designated spiritual guides that ran their community. They wouldn't make any major decisions without getting approval first. I just couldn't understand how my parents, along with hundreds of others in the group, could lose their way when it came to their freethinking.

Unlike my parents who gravitated to spiritual gurus, early in my professional career I had the unique opportunity to collaborate with several renowned business gurus. I gained insight into how these individuals applied their own unique experiences, combined with deep insights about how the world works, to coin novel concepts and create new approaches for transforming people and organizations. I worked briefly with Gary Hamel, who established the concepts of "strategic intent" and "core competencies" and has been consistently recognized as one of the most influential business thinkers of the last century. I saw how Hamel challenged the status quo at every turn, surfacing assumptions about organizations and leadership that had flown under the radar of even the savviest business executives. I cofounded a company with David Cooperrider, the father of Appreciative Inquiry, a methodology based in the field of positive psychology focused on business and social transformation through uncovering the inherent strengths of individuals and organizations. I saw how Cooperrider's unrelenting gratitude for life empowered him to see latent strengths within social systems that could be used as catalytic building blocks for positive change in even the most dysfunctional teams and organizations. Over the years, I've also had the opportunity to work with leaders from some of the world's most innovative companies, industry associations, and government organizations as a consultant and through my affiliations with business schools in the United States, Europe, and Australia—which helped me gain insight into the powerful role that culture plays in shaping mindsets and organizations.

My personal and professional experiences have helped me recognize that success depends on tapping into our strengths, gaining visibility into our blind spots, and building and deepening relationships with others. And however we define success, it's always about creating the future we want to see for ourselves, our families, our teams, our organizations, our communities, and the world. We can create our desired future more easily when we intentionally draw upon our inherent strengths while overcoming the invisible limitations created by our past. It's not always easy to do. And it can take time to learn to do. Yet, when we develop awareness of our strengths, lean into our assets, and move beyond the self-limiting beliefs that hold us back from fully embracing the whole spectrum of what we've gained from our unique experiences, we can tap into and apply a new type of intelligence in our lives—Experiential Intelligence (XQ).

The experiences that influence us can be big events, even traumatic ones, but they can also be little things that add up over time to shape our thinking and behavior. The opportunity is to embrace our experiences, decipher them, and use them to our advantage.

That's what this book is all about. My goal is to use my personal story, along with examples from my work with thousands of executives, managers, and employees, to show you how to uncover and tap into your own hidden assets to achieve your goals.

I've written this book to make it a simple read. It's full of examples to help you see how you have already acquired Experiential Intelligence just by living your life. Your XQ has given you assets that are ready and waiting to be discovered and used to create your desired future. Sometimes it takes a bit of work to find your hidden strengths, but they're there. To help you find them, I'll show you how I uncovered and then overcame certain self-limiting beliefs that were holding me back both personally and professionally. I'll make connections between my early struggles and how they shaped my mindsets and influenced my adult behavior. I'll demonstrate how to lead with vulnerability, something incredibly hard to do in today's judgmental world but a critical success factor for personal growth, team effectiveness, business innovation, and healthy organizational cultures. I'll provide you with practical tools that you can use in your own XQ development.

- **Chapters 1–3** outline what Experiential Intelligence is, why it's so important today, and how it relates to IQ (Intelligence Quotient) and EQ (Emotional Intelligence).
- **Chapters 4–8** describe specific strategies and tools that you can use to further develop your XQ by growing it in yourself, amplifying it in your personal and professional relationships, and assessing it over time.
- **Chapters 9–13** highlight how XQ applies in different contexts, including organizations, leadership, teams, and communities.

You'll see a QR code at the beginning of each chapter. Use them to view videos in which I provide an overview of what you will read, including more åof my personal thoughts about the ideas I share. You can also access the Experiential Intelligence Toolkit on my website at https://sorenkaplan.com/XQToolkit. The toolkit contains digital copies of most of the templates in this book, along with other resources. I've also made the XQ Assessment available so you can assess your own Experiential Intelligence at https://sorenkaplan.com/XQAssessment. My goal was to make this book as much of an "experience" as possible for you—because it's through experience that we develop capabilities and discover opportunities.

A final note: Experiential Intelligence is a simple, intuitive concept. The idea that our experiences shape our mindsets, abilities, and know-how is a no-brainer. And that's why it's so important. In today's increasingly uncertain world, we need simple ideas to help us understand complexity. The most powerful concepts, like our most powerful personal assets, are often those that, upon deeper inspection, we realize have been hiding in plain sight all along.

Today, more than ever, we have an opportunity to recognize that XQ is real intelligence. We all have it. And we can use our Experiential Intelligence to transform ourselves, our teams, and our organizations for personal and business breakthroughs.

Part One
UNDERSTAND XQ

1

EXPERIENTIAL
INTELLIGENCE

Chapter One Video Overview

Companies including Google, Apple, Tesla, IBM, Home Depot, Bank of America, Starbucks, and Hilton no longer require a university degree for an interview. These organizations understand that future success relies on way more than diplomas.

For a long time, a person's IQ served as the symbol of intellectual prowess and a general predictor of future achievement. Emotional Intelligence (EQ) then expanded our view of what leads to success across business, relationships, and life. EQ elevated our awareness of the importance of tuning into our emotions and the emotions of others for personal and professional growth.

People like Maya Angelou, Ellen DeGeneres, Whoopi Goldberg, F. Scott Fitzgerald, Bill Gates, Steve Jobs, Jerry Yang, Mark Zuckerberg,

Soichiro Honda, George Washington, Abraham Lincoln, Jeremy Corbyn, Russell Simmons, Rachael Ray, Vidal Sassoon, and Ansel Adams have seen extraordinary success. No college degrees for any of them.

At the same time, not all of the wildly successful people I just listed are necessarily known for their off-the-charts IQs. Nor are all of them famous for being extraordinarily empathetic, emotionally grounded, or softhearted. Some may be more intellectually or emotionally intelligent than the norm, but there are of course others who are either smarter or more empathetic. So having a high IQ or EQ doesn't perfectly correlate to "success," if you define success in the form of notoriety and achievement.

Here's the problem. Even with all the available models and measures, something's missing today that doesn't quite capture how our individual intricacies can, and do, contribute to both success and satisfaction in life. We need a way to understand how everything we've obtained from our unique life experiences—no matter how mundane or significant—holistically contributes to our ability to show up in the world and achieve our goals. We need a way to articulate and justify why we might want to hire someone who's not "officially" qualified for a job, but who we know will do a great job anyway. We need a way to recognize the inherent wisdom and strength that exist in all of us because of what we've done and experienced in both our personal and professional lives. And we need a way to make the process of understanding, appreciating, and leveraging the power of unique experiences and differences something that we embrace in our teams, organizations, communities, and personal lives.

We're on the cusp of a revolution in understanding and articulating what leads to success and satisfaction personally and professionally. We're starting to see organizations, academics, and the popular press recognize that there's a broader way to look at intelligence. We've understood for a while that we need to tap into the intellect to solve problems. We've also embraced the importance of tuning into emotions as an important tool for leading and working with other people. We're just now starting to fully appreciate that, to effectively operate in today's world and adapt to the fast-paced, disruptive changes happening all around us, we need to tap into a different dimension of our intelligence—the intelligence developed out of experience.

There's a slang term that touches the surface of this seemingly intangible intelligence: "street smarts." Street smarts is usually used to describe people with a lack of formal education to indicate they're actually "smart," but not in the traditional sense of the term. They've learned to survive in tough situations. They've developed abilities to do certain things that give them an edge in life. But even the idea of being street smart or having some type of know-how ignores the deeper process that *created* this intelligence in the first place. It's not just about the hard skills we may develop to do something; it's also about the way we think and the abilities we develop that become part of who we are as people.

Experiential Intelligence (XQ) is the combination of mindsets, abilities, and know-how gained from your unique life experience that empowers you to achieve your goals. XQ provides a holistic way to understand what's needed for success in today's world by getting in touch with the accumulated wisdom and talents you have gained over time through your lived experience.

Certain disciplines recognize the value of Experiential Intelligence without calling it XQ by name. "Extreme users," for example, are people who spend an inordinate amount of time doing something at the extreme edge of what's considered "normal." Market researchers like to talk to extreme users because their knowledge of the ins and outs of a topic runs deep from their personal experience, much more so than that of the average person.

Think about a teenager who spends hours and hours playing a favorite video game. Perhaps the situation is a nightmare for their parents, but the video-gaming teen understands the subtle nuances of the game, its social networks, its underlying business model, and probably more. The teen gamer most likely didn't learn the rules from a printed user guide, but rather from direct experience.

Or consider someone who loves coffee so much that they test a new brand every time they go to the store. They experiment with different types of bean grinders and ways to brew the coffee, including French presses, AeroPresses, handheld espresso makers, stovetop espresso makers, coffee bags, pour-overs, and siphons. Extreme users get to know something so well they become an expert by virtue of their lived experience—and not just an expert that has knowledge, but an expert who innately understands how to do something. Their abilities flow naturally.

In my own case, I became an extreme user of sorts, not by choice, but by necessity. My parents met at an event for students who had been awarded scholarships to attend graduate school at Harvard University. It was the late 1960s. My father, driven by his desire to discover the meaning of life, dove into studying theology. My mother, who attended an international high school in the Himalayas and grew up meditating with the monks, was his perfect match. She wanted to understand the common threads underlying the world's religions.

The general disillusionment that permeated their generation, combined with their intense impatience with finding their higher purpose, hit them hard. They dropped out of Harvard to live on a commune with the spiritual teacher Richard Alpert, also known as Ram Dass. I was six months old at the time. It was there that we met a guy named Danny. Danny was Daniel Goleman, who would later go on to popularize the term *Emotional Intelligence*. Goleman introduced my parents to the teachings of an Indian guru named Meher Baba, who became their unwavering spiritual focus for years to come.

We moved to California when I was three so we could be near other people who followed Meher Baba like my parents. My father, who worked multiple jobs to make ends meet and was consumed by his spiritual pursuits at nights and on the weekends, was rarely home. Just after my sister was born, my mother's mental illness emerged. Most people couldn't fathom that my mother, who had been valedictorian of her high school, attended prestigious East Coast universities, and was stunningly beautiful with an engaging personality, could become mentally ill. The slow onset of her illness, combined with the interpretation made by my parents' spiritual community that my mother's unusual behavior was an "awakening," created a chaotic and confusing home life for me and my sister. Just like how extreme users develop unique mindsets and abilities from their extensive experiences, I gained certain assets precisely because I lived in an unpredictable environment with little structure for many years.

As paradoxical as it may sound, the same things that traumatized me in my childhood also delivered unique gifts. My unusual upbringing led me to develop mindsets and abilities to adapt to my situation that still serve me positively in many ways today. At the same time, however, I developed defense mechanisms from the same process of adapting to my environment. I learned to automatically "turn off" my emotions when they became too uncomfortable. I also adopted a judgmental mindset that influenced my outlook on the world—that if others didn't do things like I would do them myself, then they were doing them wrong. My judgment *of* others protected me from my fear that I was going to be judged *by* others for my mother's odd behavior and my family's affiliation with a fringe spiritual group. I blocked off my emotions while creating a black-and-white view of the world. As a result, for many years, my "compart-mentalization" created barriers to my self-awareness and ultimately my personal and professional success. It took effort and some time, but once I was able to view my life experiences in a new light, I became more capable of seeing both my self-limiting beliefs and hidden assets all at the same time.

As I grew up and started adult life, small glimpses of the hidden strengths borne of my childhood challenges popped up every now and then. One of my first jobs was at a consulting firm that had an open office floor plan. It was a beautiful space with twenty-foot ceilings in the old Ghirardelli chocolate factory building at the end of Fisherman's Wharf in San Francisco. We named the office space "The Fish Tank" because it was simply a large room with brick walls and windows that overlooked the Bay and Alcatraz Island—plus, we had mobiles of colorful fish hanging around the room. During Fleet Week every fall, we could see the tourists wandering around far below and the US Navy Blue Angels flying high above.

With about eight of us in the office, the consultants' loud chatter filled the room each day. It was my job to conduct research and write reports for this extroverted crew. I didn't realize it at the time, but the chaotic environment of the office led me to draw upon a hidden ability that I had developed during childhood. When I responded to an email, wrote a report, read an article, or did just about anything else that required attention, I literally couldn't hear the people around me. I had learned to tune out my surroundings early in life to cope with stressful situations. Essentially, I had developed an uncanny ability to overcome chaos and distractions to focus. In one of my first performance reviews, the partner running the consulting firm specifically mentioned my unique skill as a quirky, yet valuable, ability for getting things done.

A NEW LENS FOR UNDERSTANDING EXPERIENCE

"You're the sum of your experiences" is a common catchphrase. But what does it really mean? Experiential Intelligence is much more than the set of accomplishments on your résumé. It also isn't merely what you've learned over time. Just as memorizing a bunch of facts doesn't give you a high IQ, your list of life lessons is not "intelligence" in and of itself. That's where XQ comes in.

Experiential Intelligence provides a new lens from which to view what makes you, you—and what makes your team and organization unique. It provides a framework for harnessing your past while not being bound by it, so that you can proactively create your desired future. XQ consists of three elements:

- **Mindsets:** Your attitudes and beliefs about yourself, other people, and the world
- **Abilities:** Your competencies that help you integrate your knowledge, skills, and experiences so you can respond to situations in the most effective way possible
- **Know-How:** Your knowledge and skills

When it comes to **mindsets**, you may be conscious of your attitudes and beliefs, but certain ones may be just below the surface of your awareness. Your attitudes and beliefs can either get in your way or help you achieve great things. If, for instance, you hold the belief, "I can't fail or people will judge me," then you'll most likely shy away from anything that feels risky. As a result, you won't be very innovative, as risk-taking is needed for any type of significant change. This type of belief is called a *self-limiting belief* because it limits your possibilities.

When you fully tap into your Experiential Intelligence, you're able to uncover the self-limiting beliefs you hold. As you peel back the proverbial onion, you can also discover *why* you hold the belief, and then consciously use your newfound insight to reinvent your mindset. A new, self-expanding belief can then replace the self-limiting belief, so that "I can't afford to fail" turns into "I'm comfortable with failure because I learn from it, and it's necessary for innovation."

As for **abilities**, they allow you to unite your knowledge, skills, and experiences to effectively apply what you know. Abilities are specific competencies that bridge your mindsets with your know-how. Great authors, for example, have good writing *skills*, but many authors also have an *ability* related to personal discipline. This ability is often tied to a *belief* that focus and persistence is needed to write a book. This mindset and ability lead to specific behaviors, like setting time aside to write every day and finding exactly the right words to convey the meaning they want to communicate—both of which then become skills. Great innovators often possess the ability to tolerate a high degree of uncertainty and bounce back from setbacks. Many people who have experienced hard times, big disappointments, or major curveballs in their lives and have come out the other side to thrive often have abilities tied to grit and resilience. In the business world, when we talk about someone who deeply understands how to navigate negotiations, manage the ins and outs of growing a business, and deal with demanding customers, we say that person has a high degree of "business acumen." Your abilities represent broader approaches to how you do what you do, so you can apply what you know how to do in different contexts. Your mindsets guide what you see as possible and desirable, which influences where and how you decide to apply your abilities.

Know-how includes your knowledge and skills. When it comes to knowledge, there's the information and facts you might get from school, taking workshops, reading books, or watching educational videos. That's what we call "formal knowledge." It's learned through some sort of documentation. There's also what's known as "informal knowledge," or "tacit knowledge." Tacit knowledge is learned through experience informally. Tacit knowledge often comes from doing something repeatedly over time. We learn tacitly because we spend time practicing something or in the presence of another person, absorbing their knowledge by osmosis. In the field of education, many people call this "craft knowledge"—knowledge that's developed through experiential learning activities that include practical problem-solving.

Three Building Blocks of XQ

Mindsets, Abilities, and Know-How are the Building Blocks of XQ

Mindsets, abilities, and know-how collectively comprise XQ. When we treat these components as building blocks, with know-how as the base, abilities in the middle, and mindsets at the top, we get a progression from the tangible to the more amorphous and difficult to measure. This model also suggests a progression when it comes to self-awareness. Understanding that you possess certain knowledge and skills generally comes more easily than seeing your broader abilities. Recognizing that you possess specific mindsets that influence your thinking and behavior is even more challenging.

DEVELOPING XQ IS A DYNAMIC PROCESS

We all possess Experiential Intelligence because we all have past experiences that influence where we are today. Your XQ increases as your level of self-awareness of your mindsets, abilities, and know-how increases. XQ is dynamic because how you might describe the mindsets you hold and abilities you possess at one point in your life could differ at a later point. The more you do something and have experiences in a certain area of life or business, the more you'll develop greater abilities and know-how. Your mindsets can also evolve based on insights that you gain about yourself, others, and the world in general over time.

For example, it's unusual to hold a mindset that involves a self-limiting belief like "I can't afford to fail" while at the same time tolerating an extreme level of ambiguity. More likely than not, "I can't fail" connects to a personal ability related to "attentive to detail" or "highly organized." Changing your mindsets can shift your abilities in the same direction. Alia Crum, who runs the Mind & Body Lab at Stanford University, says that mindsets can be self-fulfilling.[1] Crum's research shows that a certain level of stress in people's lives can enhance mind and body performance—*as long as the person thinks stress can be helpful to them rather than just harmful.* In one of Crum's studies, people who viewed stress as beneficial versus debilitating showed fewer symptoms of anxiety and depression, greater optimism, and improved work performance. It's a powerful concept: if you're someone who feels more comfortable when in control and your mindset shifts toward embracing more ambiguity in life, your abilities may shift away from "managing details" and toward "creativity and innovation." You get more of what you believe.

Growing your XQ is a choice that involves exploring your past experiences, understanding how you were positively or negatively impacted, gaining insight into what you're consciously or subconsciously holding onto that helps or hinders you, and learning how to frame and reframe all this to evolve your mindsets and abilities to achieve your goals.

Exploring and developing your XQ can be quite effective when done as a collaborative activity. Although you can go it alone, feedback from others, and even helping others with their own process of developing XQ, amplifies XQ for yourself and everyone involved. Early in my career, I led a small team in the change management group at HP, the computer and printer giant in Silicon Valley. Our management team decided to ditch the standard performance evaluation process because it required creating a bell-curve distribution of high and low performers. To follow corporate guidelines and do it "right," our group would have had to force some people into the low-performing category, no matter how well we did as a team or how well they had actually performed during the year. We revolted.

Instead of having individual mangers rank their direct reports, we assembled "coaching groups" that included our team members, clients, partners, and any others who had worked with us during the year. The process was simple: list examples of our work, uncover the themes within those examples that revealed the strengths of the individual, and then identify opportunities for further growth and development. Though we didn't use the words "Experiential Intelligence," the process revealed the mindsets and abilities of the person being evaluated. It also revealed opportunities for the individual to take their performance to the next level, usually through projects with the very people in the room who had just helped uncover and identify the person's growth opportunities.

The process created greater accountability to the team on the part of the individual and commitment from all involved to support the individual's development, which ultimately led to a more effective and productive organizational culture. We referred to the approach as "generative" because it left everyone involved energized and with a sense of how we were all in this personal growth process together. As our team began to experience the highly supportive and deeply transformative process, the culture of our group shifted in ways that recognized and reinforced our interdependence and collaboration. As others across the organization learned of the process, they also scrapped the traditional performance evaluation model and replaced it with ours, which began to positively impact the broader organization's culture.

Here's how Experiential Intelligence works, and how it supported our team's process:

- Experiences shape mindsets that involve attitudes and beliefs about ourselves, other people, and the world.
- Our mindsets influence our thoughts and behavior and either help us or hold us back from achieving our full potential.
- When we become aware of our underlying mindsets, we see with a new lens.

- With a new lens, we can change our attitudes and beliefs, allowing us to tap into and apply our abilities in new ways.
- When we vulnerably share our experiences with those we trust, we accelerate the entire process for everyone involved.

Experiential Intelligence is your unique internal fingerprint. No one else possesses your distinct combination of mindsets and abilities because no one else has lived your experience. But unlike fingerprints that don't change over time, you can grow your XQ.

When we understand what's happened to us using a strengths-based lens, we gain the opportunity to expand our beliefs about the past, which can influence our attitudes about the future. Instead of ruminating on the past, feeling like a victim, or thinking of ourselves as broken, we start seeing unique assets that we may have developed from our experiences. When we shift our thoughts, we shift our feelings. New thoughts and feelings lead to new behavior, which in turn will help us achieve our goals. It's easier to move through the past when you have a compelling future pulling you forward.

Developing your XQ isn't a one-and-done deal. And it's not always linear. It's an ongoing process of increasing self-awareness to identify and overcome unhelpful mindsets, and then replace them with new ones that help you tap into your hidden assets. It's a journey of advancing your personal abilities and know-how. Sometimes you might feel like you're not making much progress. Other times, you might be pleasantly surprised by the big leaps you've made in a short amount of time.

The approaches to growing your XQ that I outline in the chapters ahead include tools that anyone can use to transform themselves, their team, and their organization. While I've designed an assessment and templates using a step-by-step process, there's no one right way to develop your XQ. It may be just as valuable for you to skip around, diving into one tool first and then going back to revisit others. And these tools can be applied, put aside, and revisited over time. Growing your XQ is an iterative process, so there's no fixed timeline hanging over your head.

Humility combined with vulnerability is the fuel used in developing XQ. It starts with seeing and accepting yourself as both exceedingly capable and perfectly imperfect all at the same time. When you find others willing to reciprocate open sharing, acceptance, and curiosity, the process accelerates. Developing your XQ can become a flywheel—the more you develop it, the more you'll want to develop it further. The more you help others develop their own XQ, the more you'll develop it yourself.

CHAPTER ONE KEY MESSAGES:

- Experiential Intelligence, or XQ for short, is the combination of mindsets, abilities, and know-how gained from your unique life experience that empowers you to achieve your goals.
- Mindsets are your attitudes and beliefs about yourself, other people, and the world that influence your personal and professional success.
- Abilities are your personal competencies that help you integrate all that you have gained from your experience so you can respond to situations in the most effective way possible.

- Know-how is your knowledge and skills.
- XQ is your unique internal fingerprint—no one else possesses your distinct combination of mindsets, abilities, and know-how because no one else has lived your experience.

2

SMARTS AND SUCCESS

Chapter Two Video Overview

I t's like riding a bike."

We use this phrase to describe something that, once learned, even if we haven't done for a while, we'll know how to do when we try it again. It intuitively comes back to us. Whatever that thing is that we refer to as "like riding a bike," we've internalized it.

So, how do you learn to ride a bike in the first place?

It's simple. You just do it.

I started out on a bike with training wheels. My father took one training wheel off first so that I still had a little support. Then he removed the second wheel. When both wheels had been removed, I felt a level of autonomy I had never felt before. It took a while—including riding straight into a hedge because I froze and forgot how to brake—

but over time, I became proficient. Eventually, on weekend mornings, I would wake up early at about 6:30 AM and head a couple of miles to downtown Walnut Creek, a suburb of San Francisco, and ride in the middle of the streets. At that time, Walnut Creek was a sleepy little town, and the streets were completely empty. No cars and no people. Just me, a ten-year-old adventurer, on my bike. The meditative feeling combined with the freedom I felt cruising around, trailblazing new routes, running stop lights, and riding on the wrong side of the street still sticks with me today. My bike revealed a new world for me, both physically and emotionally.

In 1978, an English professor named Robert Kraft published an article called "Bike Riding and the Art of Learning."[2] Kraft taught at the college level and realized that his dry lectures weren't making the grade. His students could regurgitate information, but they fell short when it came to connecting that information to themselves and the real world. For instance, one student, preparing to be a high school teacher, asked for a copy of Kraft's lecture to use so the student could deliver the same lecture verbatim to his own students. Kraft realized that it wasn't "learning" that was being passed onto his student, which would then be passed onto his student's students, but rather memorized information. This insight changed everything for Kraft. He overhauled his teaching style. He became a proponent of experiential learning and wrote his famous article, which would become an important seed in the growth of the experiential learning movement.

Today, many people view experience as a cornerstone of the learning process itself. Some people refer to it as "learning by doing," while others call it "hands-on learning" or "learning through reflection on doing." Whatever you call it, when you have experiences that give you hands-on practice, you can assimilate the learning into your deeper being and then apply what you've learned in other future contexts.

It's virtually impossible to become fully adept at riding a bike without doing it. As much as someone might have explained to you how to ride by describing the mechanics of a bicycle, how to work the handlebars and pedals, the feeling of balance, and how to brake and stop, such information alone probably wasn't nearly enough—no matter how smart you are. On top of that, getting the most out of a bike, including using it safely and effectively, involves much more than the mechanics of riding itself. While the mechanics are the baseline, the best riders anticipate bumps, see obstacles in the distance that may represent potential risks, and ride defensively when traveling on the road alongside cars.

Experience is essential. And once a kid actually starts to ride, there's no going back. The ability to ride sticks for life.

Having a mindset that bike riding is a means to achieving other personal goals can reveal opportunities to use the bike in new and fulfilling ways. In my case, my bicycle served as an escape from my childhood feelings of loneliness. I used my bike as a therapeutic tool on weekend mornings, gaining control of my environment by using the blank canvas of the abandoned streets, glowing in the early morning light, to blaze my own unfettered path.

Here's a way to look at the different elements of Experiential Intelligence (XQ) in terms of riding a bike:

Know-How (Knowledge and Skills):

- Understanding how a bike works
- The skill to start, ride, and stop the bike

Abilities (Competencies):

- Anticipating bumps
- Discerning potential obstacles
- Riding defensively around cars

Mindsets (Attitudes and Beliefs):

- Even excellent riders need to be cautious when biking on the road with cars.
- Bikes provide new opportunities for transportation, physical fitness, touring, and more.
- Going on a bike ride can feel freeing and reduce stress.

The example of learning to ride a bike demonstrates something important when it comes to intelligence. First, practical experience transforms information into real knowledge and skills. The more you practice and internalize your know-how, the better suited you will be to apply your knowledge and skills in new contexts. Practicing something also helps you see connections and integrate what you know from all of your other life experiences. The capacity to discover and integrate new connections to solve new problems and do new things creates new abilities.

Yet, to really use a bicycle effectively, you need to adopt certain mindsets about the bike, other people, and the role of the bike in relation to your goals. Being attuned to others around you while biking, no matter how strong of a rider you are, is essential to keeping yourself safe. Seeing the bike not merely as a way to get from point A to point B, but rather as a tool for fitness, touring the countryside, social activity, or even meeting certain emotional needs, involves certain attitudes and beliefs that go beyond just the ability to ride. Those mindsets create new opportunities for using bike-riding abilities in new ways.

BRAINS, FEELINGS, AND EXPERIENCES

Over the last hundred years, there's been a lot of focus on the topic of intelligence. The most common measure of someone's smarts is the Intelligence Quotient, or IQ for short. The idea that we all have IQs was introduced in 1912 by the German psychologist William Stern.[3] Since then, IQ tests have become the most prevalent form of intelligence testing. Many today refer to intelligence measured on these tests as "general intelligence," or the "g factor," to describe someone's level of cognitive performance. The numeric scores that result from these tests are typically used by psychologists and educators to assess and predict an individual's current and future success.

In the early 1960s, a psychologist named Raymond Cattell introduced the concepts of "fluid" versus "crystallized" intelligence.[4] Fluid intelligence gives you the ability to see complex relationships and solve problems when faced with new situations. Cattell believed the ability to adapt to life's challenges through fluid intelligence was influenced by biology—people are born with a level of innate fluid intelligence that remains relatively constant over time. Crystallized intelligence, on the other hand, involves the ability to learn and recall information. Crystallized intelligence includes the facts and data obtained through various experiences in life. The more you practice something and retain concrete knowledge about it, the greater your crystallized intelligence.

More recently, Emotional Intelligence, or EQ, has become a mainstream concept. While the term *Emotional Intelligence* also originated in the '60s, it was popularized in the 1995 bestselling book by Daniel Goleman, *Emotional Intelligence.*[5] The appeal of EQ is that it broadens the overall definition of intelligence. Those with high EQ, it's argued, are more emotionally regulated and empathetic to others. These attributes give you a leg up in navigating personal relationships and when working in groups, teams, and organizations. EQ has become a big focus within leadership development programs in business. The more emotionally intelligent a person is, the more successful they are with collaboration and leading others. EQ filled a void in our common-sense understanding of intelligence; there must be more to intelligence than pure intellect as a predictor of success.

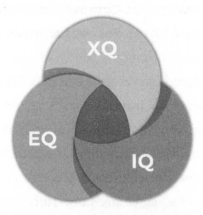

Three Complementary Intelligences.
IQ, EQ, and XQ Each Complement the Other

Success in business and life isn't just about being intellectually smart (IQ), having Emotional Intelligence (EQ), or using what you've gained from your experiences to your advantage (XQ). It's a combination of all three, and in different amounts for different people. They go together, like three intersecting circles, to help us understand what leads to success.

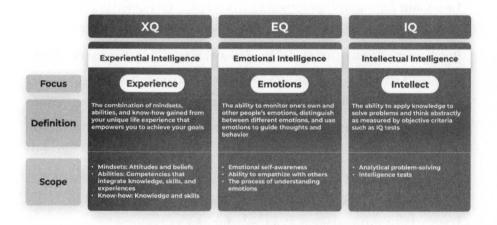

	XQ	EQ	IQ
	Experiential Intelligence	Emotional Intelligence	Intellectual Intelligence
Focus	Experience	Emotions	Intellect
Definition	The combination of mindsets, abilities, and know-how gained from your unique life experience that empowers you to achieve your goals	The ability to monitor one's own and other people's emotions, distinguish between different emotions, and use emotions to guide thoughts and behavior	The ability to apply knowledge to solve problems and think abstractly as measured by objective criteria such as IQ tests
Scope	• Mindsets: Attitudes and beliefs • Abilities: Competencies that integrate knowledge, skills, and experiences • Know-how: Knowledge and skills	• Emotional self-awareness • Ability to empathize with others • The process of understanding emotions	• Analytical problem-solving • Intelligence tests

Intelligence Comparison Chart

XQ Expands the Concept of Intelligence

While the world generally recognizes IQ and EQ as indicators of ability, the missing element is Experiential Intelligence. XQ is like the third leg of a stool that's been propping us up all along but that we haven't been able to see because it's been hidden beneath our seats. As a complement to IQ and EQ, XQ expands our understanding of what's needed to thrive in today's ever-changing, increasingly uncertain, and disruptive world.

THE SEEDS OF XQ

When Robert Sternberg was a child, he suffered from test anxiety. He struggled to perform, no matter what the subject of the test. His scores paled in comparison to his actual intelligence, and he knew it. This caused even more anxiety when he'd take tests. His troublesome experience led him to realize that tests don't necessarily tell you how smart you are—and that he wanted to do something about it.

Later in life, Sternberg became the president of the American Psychological Association and created the triarchic theory of intelligence.[6] Sternberg developed his theory to broaden the definition of intelligence itself. Triarchic theory focuses on three complementary areas that make up intelligence:

- **Analytical Components:** Problem-solving and decision-making, including understanding complex relationships, obtaining knowledge, and prioritizing relevant information to make decisions
- **Experience:** Completing tasks by applying previous experience in ways that are so natural they become automatic, or creatively applying know-how and intuition gained from prior experiences to address challenges in new situations
- **Practical Context:** Practical application of the analytical components combined with prior experience, either through *adapting* to the environment, proactively *shaping* the environment to change it, or *selecting* and moving to a better environment to meet one's needs

Sternberg's second area involving experience has been commonly referred to as "Creative Intelligence." That's because it's about how people apply the learning and insight gained from prior experiences to creatively navigate problems and challenges in new situations. Some have also referred to Creative Intelligence as Experiential Intelligence. And that's where the first academic use of the words *experiential* and *intelligence* came together in a single concept. When it comes to the definition of Experiential Intelligence in this book, XQ goes beyond just creative problem-solving. XQ assumes that our experiences impact us by shaping how we think as well as our abilities, both of which are important to understand for personal growth and success in business and life.

EVEN REALLY SMART PEOPLE CAN'T AGREE ON INTELLIGENCE

Around the same time that EQ became popular, a developmental psychologist named Howard Gardner introduced his theory of multiple intelligences.[7] Gardner challenged the idea that intelligence is simply limited to cognition. He pushed the boundaries of the concept of intelligence itself over time, listing the following types of intelligence that go beyond just intellect:

- **Musical:** Understanding sounds, rhythm, and tone, which often includes the ability to sing, compose music, and play instruments
- **Naturalist:** Understanding living things and how to work with and in nature, which relates to abilities in farming, botany, biology, environmentalism, and outdoor recreation
- **Visual-Spatial:** Visualizing the world in the mind's eye, which relates to a good sense of direction, sense of design, and visual imagination

37

- **Linguistic:** Understanding and using words to convey meaning, which includes skills related to spelling, reading, writing, and public speaking
- **Intrapersonal:** Understanding yourself, including your feelings, needs, strengths, and weaknesses, allowing you to manage your emotions and behaviors
- **Interpersonal:** Connecting into others' feelings, moods, and motivations, and using empathy to foster collaboration
- **Logical-Mathematical:** Thinking in abstractions, using critical thinking and reasoning, and applying numbers to solve problems
- **Bodily-Kinesthetic:** Having coordination, including using your body with intent and skillfully using objects and tools, which can be applied to sports, dancing, construction, the military, and more
- **Existential:** Raising and pondering big existential questions like the nature of love, good, evil, right, wrong, life, death, purpose, God, and general existence
- **Pedagogical:** Understanding how learning happens and helping others learn new things

A big appeal of Gardner's multiple intelligences is the idea that intelligence is relative. Through exposure, practice, and hard work, you can gain greater intelligence in whatever area is most important to you.

Critics of Gardner's theory say that his "intelligences" are actually "abilities." Some assert that because Gardner's intelligences can be developed, they're not equivalent to true intelligence. That argument assumes that intelligence must be innate and tied to cognitive abilities. Other critiques have focused on the difficulty in quantifying and measuring Gardner's various intelligences in light of more standardized IQ tests.

Despite the criticisms, Gardner's intelligences provide the means to stop comparing people on a single, limited variable and instead honor their unique, wide-ranging abilities—and help others gravitate to the things that both tap into their strengths and give them the most fulfillment. The different intelligences also help expand the definition of success. Even if someone doesn't score well on a traditional IQ test, they may possess "intelligence" in other areas that can lead to both personal and professional satisfaction and achievement.

Shortly after Gardner's ideas came onto the scene, Carol Dweck, a psychology professor at Stanford University, introduced the distinction between "fixed" and "growth" mindsets.[8] People with fixed mindsets assume their success is due to innate intelligence that doesn't—and can't—change over time. Those possessing a growth mindset, on the other hand, view success as stemming from continuous learning, development, and hard work. Their growth mindsets give them resolve to keep going in the face of setbacks. Whether they are as "smart" as others doesn't matter much. They may not necessarily believe that anyone can become a rocket scientist, but they do think anyone can become more successful with effort. Dweck's research adds another dimension to the intelligence debate—that your mindset about intelligence itself impacts your success, no matter how intelligent you may be. Those who possess a growth mindset are better positioned to succeed in life, both personally and professionally.

The primary reason there's debate about intelligence is because of the underlying and often unquestioned assumptions that exist about the topic. In most developed countries, the construct of intelligence is taken for granted. Five common beliefs underlie the dominant view of intelligence in modern society:

1. People are born with a certain level of intelligence.
2. Given that intelligence is an innate trait, one's intelligence level doesn't change through life.
3. Some people have more intelligence than others.
4. Greater intelligence equates to greater success.
5. Success based on intelligence equates to achievement, social status, and material wealth.

Even with the shift toward a broader, more empowered definition of intelligence rooted in positive psychology, like the ones Gardner and Dweck provide, it's still important to recognize the controversy surrounding the topic.

Why do we care so much about what constitutes intelligence and how to get more of it? The first two beliefs—that intelligence is an innate trait that remains consistent over time—naturally leads to the third belief that some people inevitably possess greater intelligence than others. If we presume that differences in intelligence come from factors outside of our control (e.g., we're born with our level of intelligence and it doesn't change as we grow older), it's easier to accept the idea that differences are simply a natural part of the world order. *Some people are just smarter than other people* might seem so intuitively valid that it would be frivolous to even question the statement.

The implication of accepting the first three beliefs, either implicitly or explicitly, is that they reinforce the logic of the fourth and fifth beliefs. The first three biologically based assumptions can lead people to rationalize that differences in socioeconomic conditions and social status are also natural, which is one of the reasons that intelligence has become a hotly debated topic.

I won't go into the various debates around general intelligence in detail. Those discussions could become an entirely separate book because there are so many contentious issues. The role of nature versus nurture is central to many of those debates. Challenges to how IQ is measured is another hot topic, including the role of implicit bias in its measurement. There's also the question about how and why the average IQ score in the United States has increased by thirty points in the last century.[9] Some have also voiced concern around intelligence tests being used to exacerbate and justify social inequities. The umbrella controversy that envelops most of these debates is whether general intelligence is a truly objective scientific measure or if it's really a social construct that reinforces dominant values and institutionalized power structures—or both.

While these debates will likely remain alive for some time to come, an opportunity exists to consciously reevaluate what constitutes "intelligence" in today's rapidly evolving world where disruptive change is an everyday experience. Arguably, it's not just intellect that makes someone successful in today's world. Resilience, creative thinking, empathy, self-awareness, and many more attributes are needed beyond just intellectual problem-solving. The debate about whether nature, nurture, or a combination of the two are responsible for IQ doesn't address the fact that we all possess both emotions and experiences. That's why Emotional Intelligence became such a great complement to IQ. EQ highlights a success factor for navigating the world that falls outside the realm of the intellect. And this is also the case with Experiential Intelligence—we all have experiences, and our experiences instill both barriers and assets for navigating the nuances of life, no matter how high our IQ score.

DEFINITIONS OF SUCCESS SHAPE VIEWS OF INTELLIGENCE

I've been fortunate to have had some profound experiences throughout my life that have shaped my knowledge and awareness of what it takes to use the past to create a successful future. I'm a firm believer that the definition of success lies in the eye of the beholder. For some, success means money and material possessions. For others, it means notoriety. Still for others, it means leaving a positive mark on the world or just finding happiness. And that's why it's important to embrace different types of intelligence—so that we don't presume that the size of our brains equates to the size of our success in business, and even life itself.

Of all the research on intelligence, XQ is most aligned with Gardner's intelligences. Although Gardner doesn't use the language of "experience" per se, the fundamental premise of his theory is that the more experience you obtain in one of the areas of intelligence, the "smarter" you can get. Experience is the common denominator. Gardner's intelligences, like XQ, provide a strengths-based understanding of people rather than pigeonhole everyone into a definition that's primarily about analytical problem-solving. People who possess different types of intelligence, like having a deep existential connection to a higher purpose and meaning in life, or being physically coordinated and superior at sports, may be as "successful"—and happy—as anyone else.

XQ also connects to Dweck's growth mindset concept. Having a growth mindset means you possess a positive, future-focused view of yourself and the possibilities for your life. XQ addresses the past, but in the spirit of gaining insight from it as a way of creating your desired future. Grounded in positive psychology, XQ helps foster a growth mindset by overcoming the impacts of past setbacks and challenges that may have cemented certain self-limiting beliefs and assumptions—which can then lead to greater self-awareness and the ability to start seeing new opportunities where none existed before, and ultimately finding success and satisfaction in whatever one chooses to do.

Developing your XQ is about knowing what you know. It involves gaining greater awareness of your attitudes and beliefs, anchored by an intention to marry your mindsets with the abilities built from your experiences to apply your knowledge and skills most effectively. But it doesn't stop there. Intelligence based on experience, which ensures resilience in today's disruptive world, also includes the capacity to adjust your mindsets over time so that you can artfully adapt to whatever your future may hold and ultimately define success for yourself.

CHAPTER TWO KEY MESSAGES:

- IQ is today's primary way of evaluating general intelligence.
- Emotional Intelligence, the theory of multiple intelligences,

and the concepts of fixed and growth mindsets broaden the definition of what it means to be "smart."

- While the term *Experiential Intelligence* originated in academic literature with an emphasis on creative problem-solving, XQ as outlined in this book broadens the definition by focusing on the personal assets developed from specific experiences that positively shape mindsets, abilities, and know-how.

- By overcoming the fundamental assumption that underlies society's interest in intelligence—that the smarter you are intellectually, the more successful you'll be—you can find greater personal and professional success.

3

THE PSYCHOLOGY
OF EXPERIENCE

Chapter Three Video Overview

Never say the word 'culture.'"

This mandate came down from the CEO of a Fortune 500 company to his executive team, which I learned about just as I was starting to advise the company on its innovation strategy. The CEO told his entire team they weren't allowed to talk about their organizational culture. Using the word *culture* felt too amorphous for the CEO, given his strong financial background. Because he couldn't adequately quantify culture and "manage" it, like he could with the company's balance sheet, he chose to ignore it. The problem was that he also wanted greater innovation and business growth. He wanted results without looking at why his culture held people back from taking risks to test out new ideas. Culture was intentionally ignored, which made it next to impossible to improve it to get more innovation.

This chapter, and the chapters following it, may challenge you in the same way that the notion of culture challenged that CEO. That's because Experiential Intelligence (XQ) can't be completely segmented into personal versus professional spheres of life. There's a psychological component necessary for understanding XQ. And that can make many results-oriented businesspeople uncomfortable.

This book applies to business, but it's also about the influence of neurology and psychology on how we define and develop mindsets and abilities—which in turn influence personal and professional success. The experiences you have, especially early in life, wire you to think and behave in certain ways. You might be able to operate sufficiently without full awareness of how you've been influenced by both the big and little events in your life. But when you show up at work, whether it's in an office or a videoconference, you're bringing your whole self to it. Especially when the pressure rises and stress increases, what you think, say, and do are often influenced by the mindsets and abilities, both good and bad, that you fall back upon. So you can choose to ignore the influences that led you to where you are today, just like the CEO chose to ignore his culture, or you can opt to understand your experiences with a new lens to make both your personal and business lives more effective at the same time.

BIG INFLUENCES OFTEN COME FROM LITTLE PLACES

When I was four, my mother showed me how centrifugal force worked by filling a bucket of water and swinging it around and around in a circle with a rope. When the upside-down bucket reached the top of the circle, my mom smiled, noting my amazement that the water didn't fly everywhere. I found it comforting. What could have ended up in chaos, didn't.

Shortly thereafter, my father and I were on a walk in the neighborhood and came upon a gutter full of soggy decomposing leaves. He pointed to the brown pile of mush and said, "Eventually, they'll all turn to dirt and go back into the earth."

Nature had rules when, it seemed to me, people didn't.

As the unpredictability of my childhood exponentially increased due to the onset of my mother's mental illness, my father's lack of presence, and my family's constant moves from one town to the next, the little scientific miracles I discovered at an early age reassured me.

I longed for predictable patterns. Would I walk into the living room to find my mother in a catatonic trance, unresponsive to the world? Would I receive a ride home from school, or would I need to walk home four miles in the pouring rain? For years, these questions, and many others like them, reverberated in my mind as a constant, stressful hum.

Finding a formula to proactively manage the social challenges of my childhood was next to impossible. Over time, I learned to deal with the discomfort of highly uncertain situations. I learned to live with ambiguity until the very last minute, then make decisions given whatever information I had in that moment. I learned to set clear boundaries with other people and to protect myself both physically and emotionally as I grew up in the world with little supervision. I didn't always have the greatest information or circumstances to work with, but I learned to make the best of what I had.

As an adult, I found a way to translate my abilities into opportunities. I realized that I was particularly adept at dealing with some of the most inherently ambiguous areas of business: how to run startups, manage corporate innovation, and transform organizational culture. It wasn't about theory. I instinctively understood how to work with limited data, check assumptions, decipher unwritten rules, hedge bets, and quickly pivot in new directions. To get to a place where I could recognize how my experiences had contributed to my strengths, though, I first had to look internally. I needed to understand the limitations that had been instilled in my psyche, along with the hidden assets that my unique challenges and struggles gave me.

The challenge for me, and for many other people, is that sometimes we have experiences, especially during childhood, that can stick with us and get in our way. These experiences may be big events, like the death of a loved one, or a series of small experiences that add up over time, like being bullied by other kids or enduring relentless criticism from a parent. As a result of these experiences, we might adopt certain self-limiting beliefs that aren't accurate or attitudes that hold us back in certain ways. To make things even more complex, sometimes highly stressful events or persistent experiences that produce sustained levels of stress can literally wire our brains to have autopilot responses to certain triggers later down the road.

When I was walking alone to school in first grade, for example, our neighbor's two German shepherds ran up to me, jumped up onto my chest, and knocked me to the ground. Though in retrospect I believe they wanted to play, I experienced them as giant, drooling beasts that threatened my life. In a single moment that lasted just a second, my brain was rewired. I lived with a visceral fear of dogs for decades. As an adult, I would do just about anything to avoid dogs, even the small, yappy pipsqueaks. I knew my fear wasn't rational, yet I felt the fear in my gut. The danger felt real for me even when there was no objective risk. For years, I subconsciously held the self-limiting belief that "all dogs are dangerous" and simply accepted the fact that "I'm a person who's scared of dogs."

At age seven, my run-in with the German shepherds felt like a truly traumatic experience. I literally feared for my life during that short interaction, which wired my brain to associate dogs with something life threatening. This process is what Bessel van der Kolk describes in his book *The Body Keeps the Score*.[10] Certain traumatic life experiences are "held" in the body and later surface as physiological responses to specific triggers connected to that original experience, like encountering certain words, sounds, smells, or just about anything else associated with it.

The thing that makes psychology complex, however, is that different people can have very different responses to similar events, even scary or threatening ones. For example, even though I experienced the "dog attack" as a trauma, a child with dogs in their household might have experienced it as a simple encounter with the neighbor's friendly canines and not have been affected at all. A similar example comes from someone I know who, at age ten, was pulled onto the dance floor at a wedding by his grandmother and "forced" to dance with her in front of a hundred people. The experience was so traumatic for him that he never danced again. For me, this would have just been a blip in my life's timeline, or possibly even a positive memory with my grandmother that I would cherish for life. Experiences are relative—they can have dramatically different effects from person to person based on many factors tied to both nature and nurture.

HIDDEN ASSETS LIE WITHIN YOUR EXPERIENCE

Think about a teacher you had, someone who mentored you, or a parent who taught you valuable lessons. You likely have had experiences with people that helped you learn something new or changed your perspective in some way that has stuck with you to this day. Or maybe you can point to an event in your life, a milestone, or something you did or achieved that gave you a new skill, new knowledge, or a completely different way of seeing the world. Making the connection between your positive experiences and the positive contributions gained from them can feel energizing.

It can be a bit harder to decipher what you may have gained from your perceived *negative* experiences. Negative experiences are just that: difficult, painful, challenging, stressful, or just overall unpleasant. Talking about these experiences with other people can feel risky. It can be a lot easier to attempt to forget about your negative experiences and try to move on. Plus, there can be social stigma tied to admitting your struggles.

Oprah Winfrey is one of a few public figures who have helped reframe what it means to reveal difficult experiences. In partnership with the psychiatrist Bruce Perry, Winfrey coauthored the book *What Happened to You? Conversations on Trauma, Resilience, and Healing.*[11] Winfrey and Perry intentionally titled the book "What Happened to You?" to contrast the typical question that people get when they're living with trauma: "What's wrong with you?" The premise of the book, and what's behind the title, is that the impact of our experiences can persist over time due to how certain events may rewire the brain. This rewiring can cause problems later in life either directly, like anxiety or depression, or through coping behaviors, like addiction. Looking at "what happened" within one's past—the experiences we had that negatively impacted us—shifts focus from pathology to empathy.

Just as it's important to have empathy for others, we need to be equally kind to ourselves when we're stymied by our own setbacks. We need to recognize that we all have our own individual stories, populated by our own unique collection of experiences, that can indeed create mountains for us to climb, but that also equip us with the tools to traverse over them. By approaching your own challenges with a recognition that you already possess strengths that can help overcome them, you have a leg up. A simple reframing of a belief can support your ability to discover hidden assets waiting to be leveraged for your benefit.

A great example of how this works comes from psychologist Richard Tedeschi. His research on post-traumatic growth (PTG)[12] addresses how even trauma can produce unforeseen benefits. Tedeschi's concept of PTG describes what happens when you undergo a significant psychological struggle that leads to a substantial mindset shift that positively transforms your life. "Negative experiences can spur positive change, including a recognition of personal strength, the exploration of new possibilities, improved relationships, a greater appreciation for life, and spiritual growth. We see this in people who have endured war, natural disasters, bereavement, job loss and economic stress, serious illnesses and injuries," according to Tedeschi.[13] He also says it's possible that, following traumatic events, "people develop new understandings of themselves, the world they live in, how to relate to other people, the kind of future they might have and a better understanding of how to live life."[14]

Tedeschi's work shows that unfortunate events don't necessarily spell perpetual doom. In fact, they may even equip you for a brighter future. Experiential Intelligence embodies this idea, though XQ applies to experiences beyond trauma as well. Embracing your XQ means looking for the unrealized assets you *already* possess and that you've developed *because* of your experiences, whatever they may be.

SHARED EXPERIENCES CREATE CONNECTION

Understanding how experiences shape us on an individual level is important. Yet we're all part of different social groups, like families, teams, organizations, and communities. When we have shared experiences with other people, we often develop similar mindsets. That's what creates culture: when people share similar attitudes and beliefs, which in turn influences people's behavior.

Shared experiences are powerful. When people are part of groups with intense shared experiences, like military units, police departments, fire stations and battalions, and hospital emergency departments, very strong cultures can result. Whole societies can also have shared experiences, like when the United States was attacked on September 11, 2001. These types of experiences can create dramatic shifts in collective mindsets almost overnight, just as PTG transforms individual mindsets.

Many organizations understand the importance of shared experience. New-hire "onboarding" programs give new employees a common experience through training, executive presentations, office tours, and other activities that reinforce the company's culture. The goal is to get everyone on the same page quickly so they can hit the ground running in the work environment. Many teams and organizations also create rituals around rewards. When someone who's done something valuable is recognized publicly, the act of doing so becomes a shared experience. Everyone who witnesses the accolades gains an understanding of what's important and valued by the organization. A shared mindset is the result, which usually leads to more of the desired behavior that was rewarded.

Team building is also a technique used by many organizations to create shared experiences focused on solidifying the culture of groups and departments. The challenge with team-building programs, however, is that they can feel contrived. Unless people feel like the program is purposeful, the team-building session can backfire by giving people an experience that instills the wrong mindsets. Experiences that are authentic, that bring people together around a common purpose, and where success is tied to the contributions of everyone involved, are often the most influential in instilling shared mindsets that influence culture.

CREATING THE FOUNDATION FOR YOUR XQ

Experiential Intelligence gives you the opportunity to expand how you think about what happened in your past and how it affected you. Even your most trying experiences, especially your setbacks and struggles, most likely helped you develop unique assets that you can leverage to shape your future.

In the broader scheme of things, moving forward isn't just about addressing past wounds. Sure, the thousands of experiences you have had in your life can impact you, stick with you, and affect your happiness, social and emotional functioning, and quality of life. And yes, some of these impacts may be bigger than others, and some may need some healing. But growing your XQ isn't about getting back to your baseline. It's about discovering and tapping into your inherent capacity for growth and resilience, and then taking yourself to the next level.

Developing your Experiential Intelligence using the techniques in this book will help you see yourself through a new lens, which will then help you view your future possibilities in a new way. That's because the concept of XQ is anchored in positive psychology, which emphasizes the strengths of people and organizations rather than what's wrong or broken. Approaches grounded in positive psychology zero in on what's working, inherent assets, and latent opportunities that exist within people and the broader social systems in which they participate. Greater happiness, well-being, quality of life, and overall effectiveness in whatever you want to do is the goal. And so, as you grow your XQ, you'll also harness the assets acquired from your most challenging life experiences, the ones that may have been weighing you down until now.

It may be necessary to heal from the impacts of an experience before being fully able to see the strengths it delivered to you. In my case, I overcame my fear of dogs using an approach called Eye Movement Desensitization and Reprocessing (EMDR).[15] EMDR rewires your brain to unpair your physical stress responses from your embedded memories of the past. The process I used first involved identifying potential "targets" that represented past experiences that caused anxiety, distress, or emotional discomfort. Given my background, I had a substantial list of targets, but agreed with the therapist that we would start with something relatively mundane for me, which was my fear of dogs. We moved into a discussion in which I provided a numeric ranking of the level of stress that the memory of the German shepherd attack caused me as I recalled it in the therapist's office. Using a long stick with a red ball on the end, the therapist moved the stick from side to side, instructing me to move my eyes to follow the ball, all the while thinking about my scary childhood experience with the dogs. We repeated the process several times until my reported stress level went to zero. At that point, we did it again, but this time I thought about the feelings of safety and confidence I wanted to have when being around dogs in the future. In what seemed like a miraculous hour-long session, I overcame my "lifelong" fear.

Overcoming my fear of dogs after so many years was a gratifying feat. After doing so, I applied EMDR to other experiences I had growing up. Yet, one thing was missing from my overall experience with EMDR. Not once was I asked to discuss or explore what I gained from the traumatic experiences that I was healing. The assumption was that the experiences injured me in some way and that the goal was simply to repair those wounds. The process left out a big opportunity: *to go beyond healing into empowerment.*

The EMDR process by its very nature, and by no fault of the approach or the therapist who implemented it, stopped short. It indeed addressed my presenting problem. But it didn't catalyze a deeper, empowered understanding of myself. The question of what unique personal assets I may have developed because of being "attacked" by those German shepherds simply wasn't part of the equation.

Through my own reflection, using meditation, and applying the tools in this book, I eventually realized that, for much of my life, I have been acutely aware of my environment. The German shepherds came out of nowhere when I was walking to school. I subconsciously didn't want to be surprised like that again. So I started noticing details. I'm keenly aware of who and what is around me. When facilitating leadership development programs of a hundred people or more, I take cues from body language throughout the room and adjust how I lead.

I chose EMDR to address my fear of dogs, but there are many other approaches I could have selected, like cognitive behavioral therapy, exposure therapy, hypnotherapy, neuro-linguistic programming, guided meditation, and many others. Depending on your own situation, any of these approaches can be useful for resetting your system so that you no longer automatically respond to certain triggers.

Growing your XQ doesn't require doing formal therapy first. The goal is simply to uncover your hidden assets and apply them to creating your desired future. It may be easier to see your strengths if you get certain obstacles out of the way first, like I did. Otherwise, the tools in this book may be enough to help you move beyond lingering attitudes and beliefs that are getting in your way.

Let's get practical and look at how to develop your XQ.

CHAPTER THREE KEY MESSAGES:

- Our unique collection of experiences equips us with strengths and tools to navigate the world, though sometimes these assets are hidden and need to be discovered.
- Experiences, especially those we have early in life, can cause neurological wiring that leads to inaccurate self-limiting beliefs or attitudes that hold us back from our greater potential.
- The concept of post-traumatic growth (PTG) highlights how significant psychological struggles can lead to positive transformation in people's lives.
- Reframing a belief can help you discover hidden assets waiting to be leveraged to support your personal and professional goals.
- When people have shared experiences, they often develop common mindsets that create bonds and influence the culture of their teams, organizations, and communities.

Part Two
DEVELOP XQ

4

DISCOVER XQ

Chapter Four Video Overview

When it comes to developing your Experiential Intelligence (XQ), you're a work in progress for your entire life, if you let yourself be one. And that's not just okay; it's a great thing to embrace. It's a counterintuitive stance to take in today's world. Being a work in progress isn't usually seen as a good thing. The term assumes that deficiencies exist. But unless you believe you're truly perfect, or that you're completely finished with your personal development, being a work in progress is a good thing. It means you're moving forward.

Your past is in your past. You can't change what's happened to you or how you've responded. But you *can* change how you view your personal history and, as a result, what you can learn from it and how you'll let it affect you. When you do this, you can also reframe your current circumstances based on your new perspective, which allows you to take a fresh look at the things you're currently doing and whether you want to change them.

You will have both positive and negative experiences for your entire life. You can choose to lean into them and embrace the surprises they reveal, or you can resist what they're communicating to you. It's rewarding to make friends with your past, learn from it, and proactively apply it to your next set of experiences. That's how you continue to grow your XQ. But you may first need to deal with your past to fully embrace your future. And to do that, you might need a little confidence in your own resilience. Having confidence gives you the courage to explore any unresolved past challenges head-on. Looking at your past won't cause you to get stuck there. If anything, avoiding the past will.

You can develop your XQ on three levels:

- **Level 3:** Reinvent mindsets (attitudes and beliefs)
- **Level 2:** Enhance abilities (competencies that integrate knowledge, skills, and experiences)
- **Level 1:** Build know-how (knowledge and skills)

When combined, all three levels make up your Experiential Intelligence. At the most fundamental level, Level 1, you could focus on building knowledge and growing skills in a certain area, like writing, marketing, financial analysis, management, playing the violin, lawn bowling, or just about anything else. There are many ways to build skills. You can enroll in a class, watch a YouTube video, attend a weekend workshop, read a book, take on a new project—the list goes on.

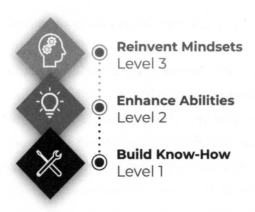

Three Levels of XQ
Develop Your Experiential Intelligence on Any Level

While knowledge and skills are indeed an important component of XQ, there's a lot more to it if you really want to develop greater intelligence. Level 2's abilities are "higher order" than concrete knowledge and skills. As a reminder, your abilities are the ways you draw upon your knowledge and skills, connect them to your various experiences, and apply them in the most effective way possible. For example, let's say you want to become a marketer. It's one thing to make posts on your social media account. It's another to create real engagement with followers, grow your brand, and generate substantial revenue from your social media marketing efforts. The former is about the skill of using your computer and knowing how to work software. The latter is about the ability to create engaging content, design pithy communications supported by compelling imagery, and connect with people on a human level through technology. To take your marketing to the next level, you may also need to figure out how to create and run a marketing consulting business, develop partnerships with other service providers, differentiate yourself from your competition, and more. Doing these things requires more than foundational technical skills. They require personal competencies like relationship building, risk-taking, and creative thinking. With these competencies, you're able to apply your knowledge and skills in ways that allow you to achieve more than basic knowledge and skills alone would allow.

Level 3 of XQ involves gaining insight into and reinventing your mindsets. As the highest-order dimension of your XQ, your mindsets include your attitudes and beliefs, both those you're aware of and those that govern your behavior without you realizing it. Examining your mindsets by studying how they were initially formed empowers you to reinvent the way you see yourself, others, and the world. When you discover the source that led you to believe something as real, you'll find that your previously unquestioned truth may not be so true after all. And when you've held a long-standing self-limiting belief about yourself, understanding the source of it can be quite revealing. For example, you may discover that it's an inaccurate belief instilled by circumstances that impacted you long ago. Making this explicit helps provide mental permission to let the belief go. When you let go of a belief, you can replace it with a more accurate one that's more closely aligned with what will serve you better in the future. The new belief can help you tap into and use your "hidden" abilities—abilities that have been sitting there all along—to do new things.

When it comes to Experiential Intelligence, your "intelligence" isn't as static as intellectual intelligence, like the kind you'd measure on an IQ test. You can develop it by focusing on any of the three levels to grow your capacity for understanding your mindsets, develop your abilities and know-how, and do all this with increasing self-awareness.

It's often by uncovering your assets that have been lying dormant that real breakthroughs can happen. Sometimes this process can occur almost overnight, as is the case with post-traumatic growth, or it can be more of an evolutionary process.

THE XQ SNAPSHOT

Developing your XQ starts with looking backward so you can look forward. I developed the XQ Snapshot as a practical tool to help you highlight your most impactful experiences and then articulate the mindsets and abilities that resulted from them. It gives you a summary of your XQ on a single page.

Growing your XQ involves shining light on what makes you tick, specifically the experiences that influenced your mindsets and led you to develop your abilities. The XQ Snapshot guides you through looking at the following in a sequential way:

1. **Experiences:** What experiences had the greatest impact on you?
2. **Mindsets:** What beliefs did you internalize from these experiences?
3. **Abilities:** What personal competencies did your experiences help you develop?
4. **Know-How:** What knowledge or skills did your experiences help you develop?

If you have had many difficult or traumatic events in life, your list will include what may seem like a large number of negative experiences characterized by setbacks or painful emotions. You might also struggle to list the abilities and know-how these experiences helped you develop. And that's okay. The goal is to get started by doing your best to list your experiences, and then to go from there.

If you would rather focus on positive experiences without considering the challenges that have influenced your life, that's okay, too. And if you have so many experiences that it's hard to prioritize which to include, consider creating two different snapshots: one for positive experiences and one for negative ones. While the XQ Snapshot template is simple on the surface, getting to meaningful answers and insights might involve a bit of reflection.

Experiences →	Mindsets	Abilities	Know-How
What experiences have had the greatest impact on you?	What beliefs did you internalize from these experiences?	What personal competencies did your experiences help you develop?	What knowledge or skills did your experiences help you develop?
1			
2			
3			
4			
5			

XQ Snapshot Template

Use the XQ Snapshot Template to Gain Insight into Your XQ

There's no one right way to fill in the XQ Snapshot. You might just start by listing some of your more memorable or poignant experiences, either positive or negative. Then move sequentially from left to right. You can also jump around if that's easier for you by filling in your know-how or abilities first and then going from there.

Here is an example of my own XQ Snapshot to provide an illustration of how experiences link to mindsets, abilities, and know-how.

	Experiences →	Mindsets	Abilities	Know-How
	What experiences have had the greatest impact on you?	What beliefs did you internalize from these experiences?	What personal competencies did your experiences help you develop?	What knowledge or skills did your experiences help you develop?
1	Traveled alone to India after college	• Norms and values differ across cultures, including definitions of "success"	• Interpret the norms and values of cultures	• Use interviews and observations to understand people & organizations
2	My father getting irritated with car salesman	• People will take advantage of me if I'm not careful	• See people's underlying motivations	• Analyzing organizational cultures
3	My mothing forgetting to pick me up from practice and school	• I need to ensure I'm self-sufficient and always have a backup plan	• Live with ambiguity and make decisions with limited data	• Manage innovation processes in companies
4	German Shepherds knocking me down when walking to school	• I'm a person who is scared of dogs	• Keen awareness of the details of my physical environment	• "Read the room dynamics" when facilitating large group meetings
5	Parents consistently unavailable emotionally and physically	• I'm not worthy of affectionate attention	• Drive for professional achievements	• Define goals, implement plans effectively

XQ Snapshot Example

Experiences Link to Mindsets, Abilities, and Know-How

A single experience can lead to multiple abilities and mindsets—some of which may serve you well, while some may not. When I was a teenager, for example, my father took me to a dealership to help me buy my first car. The experience was terrible, with tense interactions with the salesman who my father could tell was trying to take advantage of us. I would later learn that this dealership was notorious for bait-and-switch sales tactics. The uncomfortable interaction with the car salesman, even though it only lasted about fifteen minutes, impacted me in two ways. To this day, I'm apprehensive during any type of sales situation because I feel concern about being taken advantage of. The experience also led to my focus on understanding people's motivations. My ability to see competing priorities and agendas when working with teams and organizations has been a success factor as I've advised executives and led consulting programs.

If you're struggling to fill out the XQ Snapshot template for yourself, getting input from others you trust is a great first step. The best way to get started is to take a crack at the template, then share your work with someone else in your close circle. Let them know what you're doing and why, and then lead them through each experience, your resulting mindsets, and what you see as your abilities. Those we trust in our lives typically see us and value us for all of who we are, our strengths and human flaws included. You might get a reality check that you actually possess certain useful abilities you have been overlooking. Or, you might receive feedback that you hold a mindset that's holding you back. Gaining perspective on yourself from these special people can be helpful, humbling, and exhilarating.

If you're in a team or part of an organization, the XQ Snapshot is a great way to promote team building and professional development. You can decide to keep the focus positive if discussing difficult or emotional experiences isn't a fit for your style or culture. You may find that just by doing the activity, when you or one of your team members shows up with vulnerability, others will reciprocate with their own. Vulnerability inspires vulnerability, which grows trust. Trust sets the stage for vulnerability. It's a virtuous cycle.

CHOOSE YOUR LEVEL

All three levels of XQ—know-how, abilities, and mindsets—are important for developing your Experiential Intelligence. Yet Level 3 XQ, your mindsets that include your attitudes and beliefs, is probably the most powerful when it comes to driving significant change and even breakthroughs. And it's typically the hardest nut to crack of all the three levels. That's why the next few chapters focus on specific strategies for developing your Level 3 XQ.

As you move through these chapters, what you'll find is that all three levels of XQ are interrelated. By developing your Level 3 XQ, you'll likely gain new insight into your abilities, which can also help you see your knowledge and skills in a new light. The challenge, however, is that remaking your mindsets usually involves going deep. It can involve looking at experiences that elicit emotion. It can involve getting vulnerable with yourself and with others.

Some people might find exploring the deeper influences and impacts of their experiences to be an inspirational process. For others, it may be a turnoff. You'll need to decide for yourself how far you're ready and willing to go. If you're in a team and part of an organization and looking to apply XQ to your work, you'll need to decide how deep to go there, too. You might want to focus on just exploring Level 1 or Level 2 XQ and leave it at that. Doing so is completely valid and will still expand awareness about how experience contributes to intelligence. But if you want to look at yourself and your experiences in a completely new way to further develop your Level 3 XQ, the tools in the next few chapters will help you do just that.

CHAPTER FOUR KEY MESSAGES:

- You can develop your Experiential Intelligence on three levels: mindsets, abilities, and know-how.
- While all three levels are important for developing greater XQ, changing mindsets is the most powerful tool when it comes to driving personal and business breakthroughs.
- When you develop your Level 3 XQ (mindsets), you'll gain new insight into your abilities, which can help you apply your knowledge and skills in new ways.
- The XQ Snapshot is a tool that summarizes your XQ on a single page by connecting your experiences to your mindsets, abilities, and know-how.
- Teams and organizations can use the XQ Snapshot to promote team building and professional development.

5

IDENTIFY IMPACTS

Chapter Five Video Overview

t's no wonder I became adept at "reading the room" to find the hidden group dynamics at play when I work in teams.

Growing up, I was hyperalert. I had to be because I lived with uncertainty almost all the time. My mother was unpredictable. She might drive me to baseball practice, but whether she would remember to pick me up was anyone's guess. When I'd enter a room, she might be sitting cross-legged, staring into space without noticing me. Or she might say hello and ask about my day, just like my friends' mothers did with them.

My father was rarely home. I never knew when he was coming or going. And the revolving door of different babysitters spun faster than a gyroscope. I looked for cues to help me determine what was going to happen from one moment to the next. I deciphered my parents' facial expressions to help assess how well things were going. I listened for slight shifts in my mother's tone of voice to assess her mental state and what I could expect—or not—from her.

When I started working, I realized I had the ability to read people's faces, voices, and body language to gain insight into the group dynamics at play. But there was a problem: I consistently and subconsciously withheld any opinions that could be seen as controversial because I held a self-limiting belief without knowing it. I thought that if I presented ideas people didn't like, they'd judge me negatively. To top it off, I held the assumption that if I was judged, people wouldn't want to include me in their work and on their teams.

Without being aware of it, I feared the feeling of disconnection, the same feeling I felt growing up with parents who were less than present, emotionally and physically, in my life. So I subconsciously avoided reexperiencing this feeling by making sure not to stick my neck out or take any type of risk. My subconscious fear of being judged was based on the equally repressed fear that those doing the judging might withdraw from our relationship, leaving me alone and socially isolated. My fear conjured up the same visceral discomfort I felt every day when I entered the house after school. Would my mom be a normal mom, or engrossed in her world of mental illness, sitting on the couch smoking cigarettes and staring off into space? Would I feel connection, or would I experience disconnection when I said my hello? Would my father be home that night before I went to sleep, and would he be there in the morning when I woke up? My fear of disconnection led me to recreate the very thing I was trying to avoid, as I withdrew from fully participating in my business meetings.

My beliefs came from shame and embarrassment, tied to my ever-present worry that people were judging *me* for *my mother's* off-putting disheveled appearance and often erratic behavior. This belief stayed with me for decades, and I wasn't aware of it. All I knew was that I got this strange but intense feeling that I should "clam up" when sharing ideas, at least until I had some inkling that my idea was a "good" one with no risk of being off-putting to others, which usually meant it was not very creative.

Looking back now, I realize I had made connections between things that didn't belong together. I let my past lead me into self-limiting beliefs that were false. Yet, my beliefs were so deeply held that I didn't know they existed. They affected my thoughts, feelings, and behavior, which limited my effectiveness at work. And they affected my personal relationships, too. Autopilot was engaged and leading me through life, and I didn't know it.

FORECAST YOUR PAST

The concept of "forecasting the past" is simple: your past experiences influence your present thoughts and behavior. Forecasting your past involves finding the direct link between your past experiences and how they influence you today. These experiences will likely impact your ability to achieve your goals.

Forecasting your past involves illuminating specific experiences that have instilled mindsets that might get in your way of growth and success. It also involves looking at how certain experiences helped you develop strengths that you can draw upon to achieve your goals. Looking at your past in a thoughtful and methodical way empowers you to see yourself and your circumstances in a new light. And it's an essential step to understanding, appreciating, and growing your Experiential Intelligence (XQ).

By looking at your past, you can gain insight into what shaped your present thinking and behavior, and then consciously decide what to ditch and what to draw upon as you move into your future. Understanding which experiences from your past most impact your present is the starting point for growing your XQ. Whether seemingly benign events or larger traumatic experiences, in the moment they happen, it's virtually impossible to predict their later impact. Some people may respond in one way, others in another. But generally all experiences can be deciphered in retrospect. Certain events from my past, like the German shepherd attack, led me to develop personal assets I couldn't have predicted at the time. Others led to self-limiting beliefs that stayed with me for years and got in my way until I addressed them.

THE BIG AND LITTLE IMPACTS OF LIFE

There's growing awareness in research and popular culture of the role of trauma in our lives. When we experience something that produces a high amount of stress, our brains become wired to remember the experience. The neuropsychologist Donald Hebb[16] described this dynamic with the witty phrase "neurons that fire together, wire together," which explains how our neurons can be literally reoriented to produce a consistent emotional response to a given stimuli. We may or may not actually remember the details of the stressful event, but our body does. Our bodies store our collection of traumatic experiences deep within us. When we see, hear, think about, or experience something that conjures up the memory of a prior trauma, we feel and often behave like that trauma is happening to us again right then and there, even though it's not.

According to the National Council for Behavioral Health, 70 percent of American adults have experienced some type of trauma in their lives. That's over 230 million people in the United States alone. The National Council for Behavioral Health also outlines different types of traumatic experiences, including:

- Childhood abuse or neglect
- Physical, emotional, or sexual abuse
- Accidents or natural disasters
- Witnessing acts of violence
- Grief and loss
- War and other forms of violence
- Medical interventions
- Cultural, intergenerational, and historical trauma

Actors, comedians, and musicians have opened popular culture's eyes to how trauma can impact our personal and professional lives. Darrell Hammond from *Saturday Night Live*, who famously and hilariously plays Bill Clinton in many episodes, is also known in mental health circles for being the star of a documentary about his life called *Cracked Up*. Hammond's upbringing with parents who delivered unrelenting physical and emotional abuse led to his own challenges with substance abuse and depression. Hammond's documentary describes times when the comedian was about to go live on SNL but, because of an emotional trigger, could barely function. The producers and cast were quite concerned. SNL, after all, was a live show! More than once, Hammond had to be talked down from his emotional ledge to show up and perform.

While healing from trauma is obviously important, the language of trauma limits how we think about it. In today's world, traumas almost exclusively carry negative connotations. They harm, hurt, and destroy lives. While they can indeed do these things, they can also build character, foster abilities, and develop skills.

While Darrell Hammond's traumatic experiences caused struggles, they also shaped his incredible skill as a comedic impersonator because, as a child, doing impersonations was the only way he could experience a gratifying emotional connection with his mother. While he was impersonating, his mother would cease the abuse and share her delight in his humor. Her glimmer of positive reinforcement—really the only positive emotions he received from his parents, growing up—led Hammond to practice and share his impersonations over and over. The result: he became one of SNL's most prolific impersonators over his fourteen years on the show. His traumas created inner demons that required years of healing and recovery. At the same time, however, they fostered his incredible abilities that have provided him with purpose, supportive friendships, and professional success.

When it comes to the ways trauma shapes us, we need a more expansive way to understand it. I prefer the concept of *impacts*. Impacts are the specific experiences you recognize as having shaped you in some significant or meaningful way. How you view an impact can be relative because traumas can impact us both positively and negatively. The goal is to overcome the residual negative effects of your impacts while also tapping into the assets that you gain from them.

There's a difference between impacts that are truly traumatic, the "Big I's," and the infinite array of everyday experiences that can become our little impacts, or "Little I's." It's equally important to recognize that small, seemingly insignificant events can have positive and negative impacts as poignant as the big stuff. For instance, when I was growing up, my father refused to schedule time with me on the weekends. Not because he didn't have the bandwidth. He just wanted to keep his calendar free in case he got an offer from his spiritual teacher to join him for lunch or dinner. No matter what I wanted to do or how much I pleaded, my father wouldn't commit. When I was in high school, for example, my father refused to take me skiing even though we were so close to the mountains that it could have been a day trip. I couldn't comprehend why my dad didn't see me as a priority. What I did understand, however, was that my father would do anything his spiritual teacher told him to do. Knowing this, I wrote a letter to the head of the community demanding that he tell my father to take me skiing. It worked. The next weekend I was on the slopes in Lake Tahoe!

On the surface, I succeeded in achieving my goal to go skiing. But deep down, I felt disappointed that my father didn't want to spend time with me of his own volition. I internalized a message from his behavior: "Soren, you're not worthy of my attention, and I'll only spend time with you if I have to." My experience wasn't a traumatic event per se, but it was a little impact that matched a pattern of similar experiences I had growing up. These collective experiences would end up creating a self-limiting belief that would stick with me for many years: that I wasn't worthy of adoring attention. My belief played out in intense feelings of "imposter syndrome" no matter what I did or achieved. I just couldn't believe that my success, in whatever I was doing, was legitimately deserved. I never felt worthy of recognition.

Of course, impacts can also be positive. When I was twelve, for example, I spent a winter break with my grandfather, Jacques Kaplan, who was a fashion designer with a store on ritzy Fifth Avenue in New York City. He hung out with some of the modern artists at the time, like Andy Warhol, who influenced his somewhat wild fashion designs—some of which sit in the Metropolitan Museum of Art today. Jacques's customers were wealthy social elites, and he knew that crowd well. Visiting my grandfather always felt like I had teleported into a "bizarro world" where I could briefly experience an intensely creative environment coupled with creature comforts that my immediate, cash-strapped family didn't have.

One day, my grandfather took me shopping for clothes at a discount store where the cotton flannel shirts were just a few dollars each. Most of my clothes came from department stores like Sears, so the prices seemed normal to me. But what my grandfather said as we selected our shirts remains with me to this day: "The quality of these shirts is just as good as any others out there with name brands that cost five times as much, but most people think the more costly brands are better. They're all being fooled." I instantly recognized the relativity of value as a social construct: that people may eagerly pay a lot more money for things based on perception instead of reality. While I couldn't put words to it at the time, the shopping trip with my grandfather had a significant positive impact on me—it gave me insight into the dynamics of consumer behavior, which in turn contributed to my interest in sociology and psychology later in life. This little impact positively influenced my thinking, as well as my future.

My struggle to get my father's attention doesn't qualify as official trauma based on the examples from the National Council for Behavioral Health. It was a small event. Because of that, it would be easy for me to dismiss my thoughts and feelings as unjustified, blindly accepting them as normal. And for a long time, I did. These thoughts and feelings, however, stifled my effectiveness in life and business for many years without me even knowing it, and they negatively influenced how I thought of myself. So the myriad of little impacts in your life is equally important as the big stuff that happens to you.

Forecasting the past isn't just about finding the root cause of your limitations. Your experiences also give you strengths that set you up for future success. That's why parenting experts often say it can be beneficial to let your kids experience the consequences of their mistakes. It's one thing to be told to do something; it's another to internalize that insight from learning directly from a mistake. Those mistakes, however devastating they may feel at the time, can teach lessons that make kids more effective adults.

You may or may not have had a traumatic event in your past.

But my guess is that you've at least had positive experiences that have taught and served you well. Here's a simple way to think about and understand all of your experiences. I call it the Impact Chart.

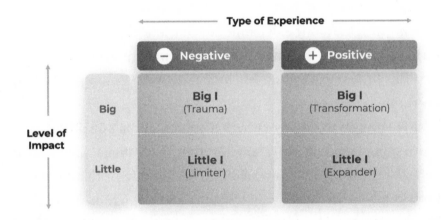

Impact Chart

The Impact Chart Categorizes Different Types of Experiences

The Impact Chart classifies the experiences that have most impacted your mindsets. There are two levels of impacts: big and little. And within each of these, there are two types of impacts: positive and negative.

Create your own Impact Chart using the template below (which is also part of the XQ Toolkit) to classify your experiences into each of the four categories. Don't overthink it. Just list specific experiences that come to mind. You'll reference this list in later chapters as you look at how they may have influenced you and how they contribute to your XQ today.

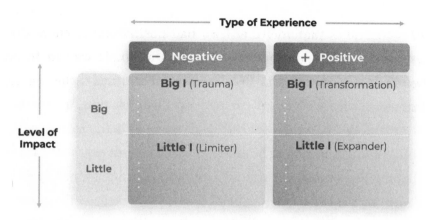

Impact Chart Template | Use the Impact Chart to Identify Your Most Significant Experiences

Negative Big I's (Traumas)

Negative big impacts are significant, often traumatic events like those listed by the National Council of Behavioral Health. They're the type of traumas discussed widely today, including different forms of abuse, significant family discord, mental illness, and events that cause post-traumatic stress disorder (PTSD). Most people are severely impacted when they experience a trauma. The feelings from the experience and the associated physical response of those feelings can stay with them for a long time, sometimes decades. Trauma can also lead to self-destructive behavior, like addiction as a coping mechanism for avoiding painful feelings.

Positive Big I's (Transformations)

On the other end of the spectrum are big impacts that have a profoundly positive influence on our lives. These are events that cause a dramatic positive shift in how we think. A trauma that leads to post-traumatic growth would be an example of this, so in this sense, trauma doesn't always have to be negative. But usually, positive Big I's are associated with positive experiences. For example, upon graduating college, I had the opportunity to travel to India. Experiencing another culture, including both the social awkwardness as well as the delightful awe of unfamiliar norms and values, shifted something inside me for the better. My "bubble" burst, and I realized there was a much larger world out there. What I had once thought was the "right" way to do things based on American culture melted away, and I became much more flexible in my thinking. I saw extreme poverty. I saw how a population three times that of the United States embraces spirituality as a way of being. My trip to India was a huge positive impact in my life because it changed my mindset for the better.

Negative Little I's (Limiters)

More prevalent than big impacts is the myriad of little impacts we experience throughout our lives. These little impacts can also be positive or negative. Negative little impacts are often the most important to understand when developing your XQ. These events may not feel very significant, and it can be hard to remember them sometimes, but they, too, can leave you with unresolved self-limiting beliefs and feelings.

For instance, although the interaction with the car salesman that I described in the last chapter only lasted a few minutes, one of the messages I internalized from the experience was that "salespeople aren't trustworthy." I consider this experience to have had a negative impact on me. While in some cases certain salespeople might not be trustworthy, throughout my adult life I have found myself overly concerned and sometimes aggressively defensive when dealing with them. The demeanor I carried around for years wasn't pleasant for me, and I'm sure it wasn't enjoyable for the many salespeople I interacted with who were just trying to provide a product or service as part of their job.

To uncover your negative little impacts, look into the past for memorable experiences, usually ones that stir up some level of uncomfortable emotion when you think about them, like fear, shame, anger, disappointment, rejection, or embarrassment. They're usually unpleasant because you carried away certain messages or self-limiting beliefs from them.

Positive Little I's (Expanders)

Positive little impacts are experiences that helped you learn something or develop a new skill. They may also have led to a shift in how you view yourself, other people, or the world in general. Because of these experiences, you changed your attitude and belief toward what feels like a positive direction for you. My experience shopping for flannel shirts with my grandfather and subsequently learning about consumer behavior from him is a positive little impact for me.

As you get in touch with your impacts, you may find that your negative impacts can be understood and reframed as positive ones. In my case, the experience with the car salesman also taught me that people are often self-interested and that finding win-win solutions in life means understanding everyone's motives. Gaining insight into your impacts doesn't mean ignoring or rationalizing your negative experiences. The goal is to learn from your experiences and uncover which impacts might be helping versus hindering you. It's possible that the impacts you list as negative on your Impact Chart might change to positive over time as you grow your XQ and discover the assets you've developed from certain experiences.

IDENTIFYING IMPACTS IN TEAMS AND ORGANIZATIONS

Identifying the impacts of the past doesn't have to stop with looking at yourself. It can also be applied to the collective experiences of your team or organization if you're in the business world. I've helped many organizations become more innovative, develop their leadership, collaborate more effectively, and change their cultures. Experiential Intelligence exists as collective intelligence in every organization. The opportunity is to tap into the XQ that resides across people and teams to create an organizational culture that leverages resident strengths and enhances overall performance.

The concept of impacts relates to organizational life because people can have various experiences in the workplace ranging from intense conflict to breakthrough collaboration. The impacts from such experiences can shape the shared culture of teams, departments, business units, or the entire organization. Little impacts regularly occur in organizations and play a significant role in shaping organizational culture and influencing performance. Simple things, like providing rewards and recognition, can create positive impacts. The leadership of one organization I advised in San Francisco identified specific behaviors they wanted to see more of from their people, such as "building efficient processes," "applying technology," and "focusing on speed."

Each quarter, people and teams who demonstrated these behaviors were given a trophy and acknowledged for their contribution. This ritual created a consistent experience for everyone in the organization and became a positive impact that communicated and instilled the attitudes and beliefs needed for success.

As adults, the experiences we have in teams, organizations, and communities can impact us, but in a different way from childhood experiences. Just like with personal experiences, your work experiences can be deciphered to give you a better understanding of the attitudes and beliefs that are at play in your organization's culture. This is important because your organization's culture can shape your own attitudes and beliefs—often without you knowing it. It's also important to recognize that the culture of your team and organization provides the social context where your individual limitations and strengths will show up, including all of the impacts that you carry with you personally. Your level of awareness of all this can play a key role in your overall success.

Negative impacts occur in organizations all the time, especially little ones. If you've ever been in a meeting and a new idea was shared only to receive a response like "we don't do things around here like that," or "we tried that before and we failed," then you've witnessed a negative little impact at work. People on the receiving end of these statements often feel shut down and may internalize the statement to the extent of withholding their ideas in the future. Others who witness the exchange are also impacted and may modify their own behavior to avoid receiving similarly stifling feedback. When these types of negative impacts consistently occur across teams and departments, the entire culture of the organization can be affected. Less frequent, perhaps, is workplace violence, which can lead to trauma, so negative big impacts are relevant for organizations, too.

If you're looking to apply XQ to your team or organization, use the Impact Chart to identify impacts that have occurred for yourself, other team members, or your team as a whole in the context of your business. It can be helpful to do this with other people so you can be sure to identify the shared impacts that have had the greatest influence on your team's performance and culture.

IMPACTS CAN CAUSE COMPART-MENTALIZATION

An insidious taboo pervades our culture: that we shouldn't vulnerably reveal our inner selves to those outside our inner circle. The taboo insists we keep our personal baggage separate from the more public spheres of our lives, especially in business. People who reveal their impacts in the form of painful histories or current-day struggles are often seen as weak or socially inappropriate. We may confide in our spouse, a relative, or a close friend, but even doing that can feel risky, particularly for men. Rarely, if ever, will we vulnerably share ourselves with our boss, coworkers, or others in our communities.

We learn from a young age to "compart-mentalize"—to moderate ourselves based on the social context we're in. It's not necessarily all dysfunctional, because emotional regulation is important to be socially appropriate and get along with others. But the result of compart-mentalization can be that we live our lives on the surface of our true selves, guarding what we say and what we let ourselves feel. It's also not necessarily a conscious choice. Sometimes we're impacted from our childhood and need to overcome those impacts before becoming self-aware that compart-mentalization is at play. Other times, we just go with the flow of the group, team, organization, or culture without questioning the compart-mentalizing influence it has on us. Either way, as a result, compart-mentalization robs us of being free to be our true, whole selves. And it deprives the other important people in our lives of the opportunity to show up for us or to learn how to support us in becoming the person we have the potential to be.

During a goodbye "roast" party after I announced I was leaving my managerial position at a big technology company, no one had anything interesting to say about their experiences working with me. Normally these types of send-offs would contain speeches with humorous stories and jokes. But I had been so measured, so protective of my image, so perfect, so in-vulnerable, that my colleagues were literally speechless. While they all said I had been "good" to work with, I realized they hadn't gotten to know the real me at all. I had been a decent manager but was far from an inspirational leader. I never tapped into my full potential, and, as a result, I couldn't draw out my own team's full potential, either. I let compart-mentalization stifle my performance without knowing it.

Our whole self shows up no matter where we are or what we're doing. It's one thing to hide ourselves from others. It's another thing to hide our inner selves from ourselves, especially when we're not aware we're doing it. Whatever we call it—denial, self-deception, or blind spots—if we want to live thriving lives and excel in whatever we do, we can't ignore the invisible barriers holding us back. This is especially true if we want to lead others in our teams and organizations to do great things together. We can't achieve greatness when self-limiting beliefs get in the way or autopilot thoughts and behaviors hijack our effectiveness.

It may seem astonishing that two-thirds of everyone in our society, on our teams, and in our organizations have experienced some type of significant, traumatic event. Most of us function just fine when it comes to our jobs. We get to work on time. We do what we need to do. We get promoted. Yet all the while, we may remain negatively impacted from some of our experiences.

We can't always compart-mentalize our inner selves when we show up at work. The baggage we carry comes with us wherever we go, no matter how hard we try to hide it. We might work in organizations with rules or organizational cultures that keep us from talking about our feelings and personal challenges. We might be able to hide the facts of our difficult experiences from others. But we can't always hide from their impacts on us. And, most likely, others can see our emotion-laden facial expressions, autopilot responses, and other behaviors that show up under stress even when we're hiding our personal stories.

It's a bit of a paradox. Arguably, work isn't the place to bring up our personal issues. But at the same time, when we go to work, we really can't help bringing our whole selves to it. Our impacts are part of us. So when we shame our impacts or ignore those parts of ourselves, we also ignore the barriers that get in our way, as well as the abilities that might be hiding beneath the surface. All this makes it impossible to contribute everything we can to our organizations. And if you're leading a team or are part of a team, and you're not tapping into the whole of everyone's experience, you're leaving a lot of unused assets on the table.

Let's look at how to discover your XQ, and that of your team and organization, so you can work with your impacts to develop greater Experiential Intelligence.

CHAPTER FIVE KEY MESSAGES:

- *Impacts* are specific experiences that have shaped your mindsets and abilities in some meaningful way.
- There are four types of impacts that influence the XQ of individuals, teams, organizations, and communities: Traumas, Transformations, Limiters, and Expanders.
- Compart-mentalization occurs when you consciously or subconsciously constrain how you show up in some social contexts versus others due to your impacts.
- Compart-mentalization can be functional in that it allows you to cope with difficult emotions, but it can also stifle your performance and reduce satisfaction and overall success in your personal and professional lives.
- Impacts shape the shared culture of teams, departments, business units, and the entire organization.
- When you decipher the impacts of your team and organization, you're better able to understand your culture, overcome hidden barriers to performance, and leverage strengths that take you and your teammates to the next level.

6

DECODE MINDSETS

Chapter Six Video Overview

Virtually everyone has experienced challenging events in their lives. While not everyone has experienced a trauma, just about everyone has experienced emotionally grueling setbacks or struggles at some point or another. And for those that say they haven't, they probably have and are simply protecting themselves from acknowledging the difficult emotions tied to those experiences.

Negative experiences are often the most influential when it comes to instilling attitudes and beliefs that don't serve us well. So, it's important that we understand their impact on us so we can move through any residue that needs cleaning up and take our Experiential Intelligence (XQ) to the next level.

MINDSETS DEFINE YOUR REALITY

Where do mindsets come from? They're built over time from our experiences in our families, friend groups, social media networks, organizations, communities, and society at large. Our experiences, especially early in life, create and reinforce our mindsets. That's why people from different countries usually hold different culturally informed attitudes and beliefs. And even within a specific culture, people from different families can have different mindsets. We can develop mindsets with attitudes and beliefs about anything—people, brands, companies, political parties, social and environmental causes, and more.

Mindsets exist at the individual level, but on a macro level they're reinforced through social interactions. When people share similar self-limiting beliefs and are part of the same team, organization, or community, their collective mindsets shape their "sub-culture." Dysfunctional organizational cultures often contain unquestioned attitudes and beliefs that limit performance. In organizations that perpetuate self-limiting beliefs, we often hear people say things like, "It's just not done that way around here," or "We can't because it's not in our scope," or "We need more data before we can do anything." These beliefs are perfectly designed to stop change and hinder progress.

When you go about life unaware of your mindsets, you're essentially operating on autopilot. Your thoughts, decisions, and even feelings are influenced in ways that fly under your radar. Gaining greater awareness of your mindsets gives you more control over what you do, how you do it, and how successful you are when you do it. You're better able to achieve your personal and professional goals when you know what influences you and why, as everything will become more conscious and intentional.

DECODE YOUR MINDSETS

Growing your Level 3 Experiential Intelligence involves developing awareness of how and why you think the way you do because of your experiences. It takes humility to look at yourself in the mirror so you can see yourself in a new light. Developing your mindsets means growing your capacity for understanding what makes you tick—the attitudes and beliefs that guide what and how you think, feel, and act. To achieve this, you need to uncover the source of any self-limiting beliefs.

Becoming aware of your mindsets delivers an entirely new level of self-awareness. New mindsets allow you to do things differently, helping you further develop your abilities and know-how in ways you didn't realize you could before. It's the positive feedback loop of XQ development.

The Beliefs Mapper is a simple tool that provides a step-by-step structure for decoding why you believe what you believe. Like the XQ Snapshot, the Beliefs Mapper begins with the experiences that you believe have had the greatest influence on you. There are three steps in the process: listing your impacts, identifying the messages those impacts imparted to you, and determining what beliefs you internalized from these messages.

1. Identify Influential Impacts

Again, your impacts are the experiences that have had the greatest impact on your life. Start by listing your most influential impacts on the Beliefs Mapper template. Reference the impacts you may have listed in your original XQ Snapshot and Impact Chart. When decoding your mindsets, however, you'll get the most bang for your buck by focusing on negative impacts. Getting in touch with your negative impacts isn't about finding things to complain about or make you feel bad. It's about determining what you can learn from the most. Negative impacts are your most poignant experiences that contain unresolved feelings or that don't sit right with you when you think about them, even though they might have occurred many years ago.

Impacts can be single, isolated events that happened in your life. Or they can be a set of experiences you've had over time that, to you, feel like they merge into a broader, unified category of experience. Some examples of my own impacts include my father's lack of prioritization in spending time with me, like when he refused to take me skiing and when we had the uncomfortable interaction with the car salesman.

2. Decipher Your Messages

Big and little impacts contain messages. Sometimes an impact's actual event and its corresponding messages are literally the same, like when an older sibling, parent, or manager criticizes you. Other times, you might have interpreted messages from others' behaviors. When my father rejected my requests to take me skiing so he could keep his weekends free for his spiritual teacher, for instance, I interpreted his behavior as communicating, "You're not a priority for me." The interaction with the car salesman sent a message to me that was never said aloud but that I internalized as "people trying to sell you things aren't trustworthy."

For each of your impacts, list the specific messages that you believe were conveyed to you through your experience. Consider the message that was either said to you directly or that you interpreted from the impact you listed.

3. Bare Your Beliefs

Beliefs are your truths. They're your convictions about reality. They help you make sense of why things work the way they do.

The third step in decoding your mindsets is to identify your self-limiting beliefs. By looking at the messages you received from your impacts and connecting them to the belief(s) they led you to adopt, you can start to see the collective beliefs that shape how you think.

Your beliefs make up your mindsets. And your mindsets guide how you operate in the world. That's why it's possible to walk around with self-limiting beliefs that affect your relationships and success without knowing it. And that's also why recognizing your self-limiting beliefs is an essential step toward reinventing them, so you can in turn reinvent your mindsets.

Self-limiting beliefs stifle your full potential. For example, the self-limiting belief that "I can't fail, or else people will judge me" has a very different effect than that of its opposite, self-expanding belief:

"I'm comfortable with failure because I learn from it, and it's necessary for innovation." Self-limiting beliefs hold you back from either trying something new or achieving optimal performance in whatever you're already doing. That's because we relate to our beliefs as truth. We don't view our beliefs as the subjective interpretations they are. We believe they are reality, which is why they can so easily get in our way.

In my case, my self-limiting belief as a result of my experience with my father was the generalization that I'm not worthy of attention. The self-limiting belief tied to my experience with the car salesman was "I must always question other people's motives." Beliefs can be about anything. The best understanding of a self-limiting belief comes from articulating it from your perspective using an "I" statement, since it's your own personal belief.

To put self-limiting beliefs in context, I've created what I call the Mindset Map, which characterizes how your beliefs show up consciously and subconsciously. The map outlines whether the belief is negative (it holds you back in some way) or positive (it supports you in some way) and conscious (you're aware of it) or subconscious (you're unaware of it). Depending on where the belief falls on the map, it's characterized as one of four types:

1. **Negative Self-Talk:** Negative beliefs that become conscious self-talk that constrains your potential
2. **Self-Limiting Beliefs:** Negative beliefs you're unaware you hold that constrain your potential
3. **Positive Affirmations:** Positive beliefs that become pos-

itive affirmations you tell yourself that support your potential

4. **Self-Expanding Beliefs:** Positive beliefs you're unaware you hold that grow your potential

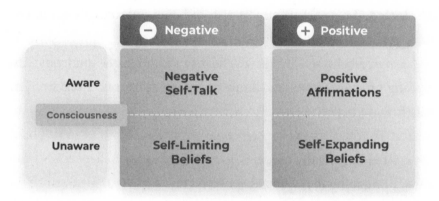

The Mindset Map

The Mindset Map Classifies Different Types of Beliefs

When you're aware of your positive beliefs, they essentially become positive affirmations. They're ideas that validate your strengths and provide reassurance that you have an asset you can use to achieve your goals. On the flip side, negative beliefs that you're aware you possess become negative self-talk because if you know you hold them, they consciously confirm you possess some type of inherent limitation.

The beliefs that lie just below your everyday awareness are either self-limiting or self-expanding beliefs. They're subconscious until you become aware of them. Becoming aware can be rewarding whether they are positive or negative because gaining self-insight is empowering. Identifying your self-limiting beliefs is the first step in replacing them with beliefs that better serve your goals.

Although everyone possesses a unique set of life experiences, many people share similar self-limiting beliefs. Some of these beliefs can include being unworthy, at risk of being judged, or less capable than others. Recently, our society has started to recognize some of these shared beliefs, which is why terms like "imposter syndrome" are gaining broader awareness. Some of the most common self-limiting beliefs include:

- I'm not worthy of...
- I'm going to be judged, so I won't...
- I can't fail, so I won't...
- I'm not as good as them, so I can't...
- I'm not smart enough, so I can't...
- I can't because I'm not...
- I'm afraid of...

The result of these beliefs is always the same: they invade your thoughts and stop you from taking steps toward the things you want to do by telling you that you can't or shouldn't do them. They may stop you from trying something new, such as starting a business, taking on new responsibilities in your current role, or asking your team to take a risk. Self-limiting beliefs distract you, delay your efforts, and deal doses of self-doubt.

Complete the Beliefs Mapper template to the best of your ability by listing the self-limiting beliefs you internalized from the messages you received. I've included a couple of my own responses in the template so you can see how the process works:

Impacts →	Messages	Beliefs
What experiences most impacted me?	What message did I receive?	What "truth" did I internalize?
1	• My father wouldn't take me skiing	• You're not a priority for me	• I'm not worthy of attention
2	• Uncomfortable interaction with the car salesman	• People trying to sell you something aren't trustworthy	• I must always question other people's motives
3			
4			
5			

Beliefs Mapper Template

Use the Beliefs Mapper Template to Decode Your Mindset

REMAKE YOUR MINDSETS

Now that you've filled in your Beliefs Mapper, take a step back and take it in. Look at the experiences you just listed. Most likely, these experiences have had the greatest impact on your life. They've influenced your perspective on the world. They've shaped your responses to your other experiences. They've influenced your success.

The opportunity now is to replace your self-limiting beliefs with self-expanding beliefs, which is the last step in the process of decoding your mindsets.

In my case, I decided to share what I saw as the impact of my father's behavior on me with several trusted friends, as well as my wife. I obtained external feedback and validation that the messages and self-limiting beliefs I took away from my experiences made perfect sense, given what I'd been through. I received empathy from others, but also a reality check: no one agreed that my self-limiting belief that I wasn't worthy of attention was valid. They weren't talking about attention in the form of fame or social media followers. They reassured me that, as a human being looking for love and connection, I was as worthy as anyone of receiving these things. I also approached my father and requested we meet over coffee so I could share a few thoughts about my experience growing up. We ended up having several conversations about our relationship, and he acknowledged the impact he had on me. My self-limiting belief dissolved over time, and it was replaced by its opposite belief: *I'm worthy of having mutually beneficial, connected relationships.*

If you get rid of one belief, it's typically replaced by another. If you stop believing the world is flat, for example, you'd likely need to replace it with another belief, like that the world is round. But how do you know what to replace your self-limiting beliefs with?

Inspired by research from Jeremy Clifton at the University of Pennsylvania,[17] I created a template I call the Beliefs Expander that can help you remake your mindsets more intentionally than letting it happen by chance. Clifton and his colleagues—including

Martin Seligman, the founder of positive psychology, and Carol Dweck—have been developing and empirically validating a list of "Primal World Beliefs" that they say underlie people's happiness and well-being.

The Primal World Beliefs model includes beliefs that impact people's outlook on life. Most of the beliefs "ladder up" to three high-level beliefs: safe (versus dangerous), enticing (versus dull), and alive (versus mechanistic). These three beliefs also ladder up to a single overarching worldview—that the world is either good or bad. It's an intuitive model, given that we already have terms for optimistic versus pessimistic people who respectively see the glass as half full (i.e., the world is positive) or half empty (i.e., the world is negative). As you read through the beliefs, you'll see they are written in the positive tense. The "Safe vs. Dangerous" belief, for example, is explained as "The world is safe, comfortable, stable, and fair; there is rarely cause for worry." The negative spin on this definition would be "The world is not safe, comfortable, stable, or fair; there is frequently cause for worry."

The negative version of each belief can be considered a self-limiting belief. The positive version is a self-expanding belief. For example, the beliefs that the world is either "meaningful" or "meaningless" are positive and negative, respectively. If you internalize the belief that "the world and basically everything in it matter a great deal," you open yourself up to new possibilities to discover meaning everywhere you look. If you've internalized that the world is meaningless, on the other hand, your motivation to broaden your horizons will be limited because you hold the assumption that whatever you find won't be of much value.

Good vs. Bad

When the world is seen as good, it is a delightful place that is beautiful, fascinating, safe, abundant, full of meaning, improvable, and getting better. When the world is seen as bad, it is miserable, dangerous, ugly, meaningless, barren, impossible to change and getting worse.

Safe vs. Dangerous
The world is safe, comfortable, stable, and fair; there is rarely cause for worry.

Pleasurable vs. Miserable
Most things are typically enjoyable

Regenerative vs. Degenerative
The world's natural tendency is to heal/stabilize vs. weaken/decay

Progressing vs. Declining
The world is getting better instead of worse.

Harmless vs. Threatening
The world and most things in it are typically not very dangerous

Cooperative vs. Competitive
The world runs on trust and teamwork, not brutal competition

Stable vs. Fragile
The world and most things in it are resilient instead of frail or easily destroyed

Just vs. Unjust
The world is a fair place where you typically get what you deserve

Enticing vs. Dull
The world is beautiful, fascinating, meaningful, brimming with opportunities, and worth exploring; there is rarely cause for boredom.

Interesting vs. Boring
The world and most things in it are fascinating and intellectually engaging

Beautiful vs. Ugly
The world and most things in it are beautiful and aesthetically engaging

Abundant vs. Barren
The world is a promising place full of opportunities and resources

Worth Exploring vs. Not Worth Exploring
Everything is worth trying or doing, at least once

Meaningful vs. Meaningless
The world and basically everything in it matters a great deal

Improvable vs. Too Hard to Improve
Most things can be readily changed for the better

Funny vs. Not Funny
The world is full of humor everywhere you look

Alive vs. Mechanistic
The world is intentional and interactive; the universe reveals purpose and messages everywhere.

Intentional vs. Unintentional
Most things happen for an underlying reason

Needs Me vs. Doesn't Need Me
Everyone is alive and on earth for a reason

Interactive vs. Indifferent
Everyone can make a difference every day

Primal World Beliefs | Identify the Beliefs That You Hold

Review the list of beliefs above and see if you listed any of the negative ones as your own self-limiting beliefs on the Beliefs Mapper template. If so, you might get an instant clue as to what your self-expanding beliefs are, since they would be the opposite of your self-limiting beliefs. Either way, create a list of your self-limiting beliefs on one side of the Beliefs Expander template below, and your self-expanding beliefs you will replace them with on the other. You might get inspiration from the Primal World Beliefs or even use them directly.

Self-Limiting Beliefs	Self-Expanding Beliefs
What beliefs hold me back?	What beliefs can I replace them with to expand opportunities?

Beliefs Expander Template
Use the Beliefs Expander to Remake Your Mindset

TAKE YOUR TIME

Don't feel like you need to rush things. It may take you days, weeks, or even months to feel like you've adequately completed the templates in this chapter. In our culture of fast food, overnight delivery, and instant access to just about everything, it's natural to want a quick fix. Don't sweat it if it takes you time to get to a place where you feel like your Beliefs Mapper and Beliefs Expander templates really represent your beliefs and goals.

My own process of identifying my self-limiting beliefs was gradual and occurred over a few years. That's the case for a lot of people, though some people might have a significant or poignant experience that reveals their beliefs more quickly, like in the case of post-traumatic growth. For most people, however, the process can take time.

If you want to accelerate things and challenge yourself, then confide in someone you trust, letting them know you're looking at yourself to try to improve and develop. It might be tough to do, but it's a tried-and-true way to help you get unstuck, see things differently, and shift your thinking. It can be quite difficult to see your self-limiting beliefs on your own; others generally see them better than we do ourselves. But it can take humility to hear what they have to say.

Share what you see as your impacts, their messages, and your self-limiting beliefs. Then ask what they think. Ask if they think your assessment is accurate based on what they know about you. Ask if they, too, recognize the beliefs you listed. Get their input on what self-expanding beliefs might benefit you most. Using your trusted network in this way will help you see your internal self more clearly.

Once you've completed your templates, you may want to go back and revisit your XQ Snapshot and revise it according to any self-limiting beliefs you've now surfaced. Your insights may provide a new lens with which to identify the know-how, abilities, and mindsets that you can leverage.

CHAPTER SIX KEY MESSAGES:

- Mindsets are molded over time from experiences within families, friend groups, social media networks, teams, organizations, communities, and society at large.
- The impacts from experiences deliver messages that are internalized as attitudes and beliefs that become the foundation of mindsets.
- Self-limiting beliefs are any thoughts that stifle you from achieving your full potential and often include beliefs about being judged, unworthy, incapable, or fearful of something.
- Growing your XQ involves developing awareness of the attitudes and beliefs that guide what and how you think, feel, and act, and then replacing them with self-expanding beliefs that help you tap into your hidden strengths to achieve your goals.

7

REINVENT RELATIONSHIPS

Chapter Seven Video Overview

During the summer before I started second grade, my sister and I spent two weeks with my grandfather at a small condo on the shores of Lake Tahoe. At the end of our trip, my parents made the four-hour drive from the San Francisco Bay Area to pick us up and take us home. We hadn't seen our parents in what seemed like an eternity, so we eagerly awaited their arrival. I'll never forget the moment when they knocked on the door and burst into the living room with an enthusiastic "Helloooo!"—their arms raised high and ready for hugs. My mother walked right past me and embraced my sister, ignoring me as if I were invisible. Not a word. Not even a nod my way. My smile soon flipped to a frown, and then the tears came.

My mother's schizophrenia had really kicked in around that time, and her inexplicable behavior was the result. When she ignored me, I ran away. Literally. I ran out the door and down the stairs of the second-floor condominium, winding through the paths of the complex. My grandfather trailed behind, eventually catching up to me. He scooped me up in his arms and carried me back into the condo.

For thirty-five years, my somewhat fuzzy memory of this event focused on my anger toward my grandfather, who I felt had hurt me by chasing me down and bringing me back to the condo. Just before my grandfather passed away, however, he empathetically mentioned how difficult it must have been when my mother treated me in such a confusing and upsetting way that summer. I realized in that moment that my memory and feelings surrounding the event were inaccurate. At the time, I couldn't see or take in the full experience of what had happened to me. The reality of the situation was that my grandfather's actions were an expression of love and protection.

VISCERAL MEMORIES ENGAGE AUTOPILOT RESPONSES

Autopilot responses are thoughts, feelings, and behaviors that automatically arise when we're triggered. Just like a physical knee-jerk response when the patella of our knee is whacked by the doctor, our reactions can be instantaneously unintentional when we're reminded of our negative impacts. If we want to understand our autopilot responses and work to overcome them, we need to analyze what triggers them.

You may not consciously recall a specific impact from your past when you're triggered, but the message you received from it long ago, which lies deep within you, pops up like a whack-a-mole. The message can also elicit the self-limiting belief that's tied to it, usually in one fell, subconscious, split-second swoop. It's similar to when we smell something and a memory instantly transports us back to the past, and we feel the feelings we had when we first smelled it.

These responses—which I simply call *autopilots*—all work the same way: we get a jolt of the past that results in spontaneous thoughts, feelings, or behaviors. For a split second, autopilot takes over due to a "visceral memory." We then react and say or do something without thinking. Each of our visceral memories involves a discrete bundle of related experiences, messages, and self-limiting beliefs that can instantaneously cause an autopilot reaction when activated.

Autopilots can occur as a response to painful or unpleasant self-limiting beliefs. And we might react by showing judgment, defensiveness, or anything else to avoid facing those self-limiting beliefs. In other cases, autopilots result from fear of not getting our needs met or of the possibility of an unacceptable event happening in the future. By first understanding our self-limiting beliefs, we can gain insight into the autopilots that protect us from facing them head-on. And once we understand our autopilots, we'll be better able to see how they show up and influence our relationships.

To this day, when I have an interaction that hurts in some way, my gut instinct is to retreat—to withdraw and protect myself from further emotional pain. I feel the instinct to run away, just like I did when I was seven years old at Lake Tahoe. It's a visceral memory and autopilot response connected to the self-limiting belief that if I continue participating in a difficult, emotionally charged discussion, then I won't get my needs met. My self-limiting belief tricks me into believing that if I remain in the conversation, I can expect more hurt, which is something I subconsciously don't want to happen. So my autopilot response is the compulsion to depart from the interaction physically and emotionally. I'm continually working to recognize this autopilot when it's about to become engaged. I've learned to recognize my visceral memory and consciously self-reflect in the moment it's triggered so I can more effectively move through emotionally charged conversations without running away, both figuratively and literally.

The Autopilot Mapper is another template like the Beliefs Mapper, but with autopilots in the last column. You can use the same inputs from your Beliefs Mapper if you've already created it, or you can take this template and map it all—your impacts, messages, self-limiting beliefs, and autopilots. Try working linearly, tracing the path from impact to autopilot. If you get stuck, sometimes it can be easier to list an autopilot and then go in reverse order, looking at the self-limiting belief behind it, the message that's behind that, and then the impact behind the message.

Impacts →	Messages 💬	Beliefs ☁	Autopilots 🎛
What experiences most impacted me?	What message did I receive?	What "truth" did I internalize?	What do I automatically think, feel, or do?
1			
2			
3			
4			
5			

Autopilot Mapper Template | Use the Autopilot Mapper to Identify the Drivers of Your Autopilot Responses

When exploring your autopilots, it can be helpful to ask someone you trust the following questions for a reality check. The language of the questions may need to be adjusted based on how well or long you have known the person, so modify these as needed:

- Do you ever see me react before thinking, and what do I usually do when that happens?
- What's going on in the interaction or conversation right before I react in this way?
- What is the impact that this reaction has on you or other people?

Don't worry if you can't drum up an autopilot for a given experience. Just fill in what you can. The process may take time, and it's also possible that you might not have autopilots connected to every impact and self-limiting belief.

EQ AND XQ REINFORCE EACH OTHER IN RELATIONSHIPS

According to Daniel Goleman, emotionally intelligent people are both aware of and able to control their emotions. As a result, people with high Emotional Intelligence (EQ) are better able to temper their autopilot responses. Because autopilots are often connected to a belief that conjures up an emotion, being aware of your emotions makes you better equipped to spot your autopilots. People with high EQ also empathize well with others' emotions, which can help foster and grow relationships more easily.

Sharing your stories with others can foster greater awareness of your own beliefs. Richard Tedeschi highlights the importance of "disclosure" when it comes to overcoming the negative effects of trauma. In his popular Harvard Business Review article "Growth After Trauma," Tedeschi describes disclosure as the process of sharing "what has happened and is happening: its effects—both small and broad, short- and long-term, personal and professional, individual and organizational—and what you are struggling with in its wake."[18] Vulnerability and disclosure don't just benefit those dealing with some type of trauma. When you share your thoughts and feelings about your prior experiences, as well as their impacts on you in the present day, you can inspire others to share their own experiences. This mutual sharing builds trust and deepens relationships, especially when both parties approach the process with curiosity and empathy.

Reflecting upon your past experiences often elicits emotion. When you have awareness of your emotions, especially difficult and uncomfortable ones, you can process them through opening up to others you trust, which helps dissipate whatever stranglehold these emotions may have on you. And when you're tuned into others' feelings, you can support their own emotional processing. Through neutralizing the negative emotional content of our past experiences, we can more objectively look at the circumstances surrounding our past events and the impacts that may have resulted. Thus, developing your *Emotional* Intelligence accelerates the growth of your *Experiential* Intelligence.

Daniel Goleman says that one of the best ways to grow your EQ is through meditation. One of the other benefits I've personally experienced from meditating is gaining greater awareness of my beliefs, which makes it easier to decide which beliefs to keep and which to ditch. Through meditation, you can more consciously replace self-limiting beliefs with self-expanding beliefs.

Beliefs and emotions often go hand in hand. If you hold a self-limiting belief, and you're reminded of it through an interaction you have, you'll likely experience the same emotion you had when that belief was instilled within you. It's also possible your belief-emotion sequence will lead to some type of autopilot response. This is a similar dynamic to—though not necessarily as extreme as—what Bessel van der Kolk outlines in *The Body Keeps the Score* when he describes how people have automatic behavioral responses from PTSD.

REVEAL YOUR RELATIONSHIP LOOPS

When you're involved in relationships with other people that elicit the same self-limiting beliefs and emotions over and over again, they can make us feel like we're stuck. This can happen in one-to-one relationships, but also in teams and organizations. It's like the movie *Groundhog Day*. We have an experience that repeats itself with the same players, and no matter what we do, it seems like we can't change the script. The good news is that there are ways to create a new storyline and reinvent your *relationship loops*.

Once you understand your internal processes—impacts, self-limiting beliefs, and autopilots—you can more easily see how they influence your existing relationships, as well as how those relationships may be reinforcing your self-limiting beliefs and autopilots. To sufficiently assess where you need to free yourself up to more effectively grow your XQ, it's important to examine your current relationship dynamics to understand if and how they may be impeding your goals.

Relationship loops are patterns within our current relationships that reinforce specific thoughts, feelings, and behaviors perpetually over time. There are both positive and negative relationship loops.

Negative relationship loops reinforce thoughts, feelings, and behaviors that don't serve your goals. They can leave you feeling defensive, dejected, and depleted. Sometimes it's hard to recognize you've been participating in a negative loop. There can be an element of codependence that characterizes negative relationship loops, such as feeling personally responsible for the feelings or actions of a loved one or your team. We may remain in these loops because we believe, consciously or subconsciously, that we have no choice but to continue participating in them. We might feel the dysfunction, but we can't see a way out.

On the other hand, positive relationship loops involve one-on-one and group interactions that tap into our strengths and inspire us to do new things. As a result, our skillsets and mindsets evolve, and our abilities strengthen. High-performing teams use positive loops to innovate, push themselves to achieve challenging goals, and create organizational cultures that perpetuate success. In fields like education, these types of relationships are referred to as "generative." Positive loops leave you feeling good, like you've enhanced your life and advanced your goals.

Early in my career, I started a consulting firm with a business partner named Drew, a marketing expert who could artfully land new consulting business with his charming English accent and dry sense of humor. He also managed our accounting, taxes, insurance, and just about everything else needed to run our small business. However, when we won a client project, I often led the work because I had a unique ability to facilitate meetings, create insightful research reports, and build relationships with top executives. At the end of our projects, many clients wanted me to stick around as an adviser.

It took me ten years to recognize that Drew and I were stuck in a negative relationship loop. The loop started with my misperception that Drew wasn't contributing equally as a partner in our firm. After all, I was the one that most of our clients wanted to lead their projects. I was the one who ensured we got repeat business. As a result, I was consistently irritated with him, using a sharp tone of voice and subtle condescension whenever I deemed that the quality of his consulting work didn't match mine. I treated Drew in a way that didn't acknowledge his unique and important contributions. Drew most likely saw me as short-tempered and arrogant, but he never said a word about it. He just accepted my un-partner-like behavior. For years, we played out the loop over and over again.

Even though we had a financially successful firm and were doing meaningful work, I felt dissatisfied. My self-limiting belief was this: *if others can't do what I do equally well, I'm better and more valuable than they are.* Eventually, I recognized that Drew's unique abilities to build new business and run our company, skills I hadn't yet acquired on my own, were equally as valuable as my skillsets. I recognized my self-limiting belief that caused me to feel constant irritation. I no longer wanted to live with a constant hum of irritation in my interactions with such an important person in my life. I wanted a relationship where feelings of appreciation and gratitude flowed to inspire creativity instead of resentment, yet I hadn't recognized how I was keeping us from having that. Fortunately, Drew and I reinvented our loop during the last few years of working together before he retired, and we remain friends today.

Relationship loops get reinforced over time, which is why we can start feeling increasingly frustrated with our families, teams, and organizations. We may not realize how dissatisfied we are or how dysfunctional things have been until some type of crisis or explosive interaction occurs. The dysfunction creeps up on us over time, incrementally getting worse, all the while reinforcing the long-standing self-limiting beliefs we've held for years. Because these relationships feel familiar and therefore misleadingly "normal," we endure them until something jolts our awareness, causing us to suddenly see our situation, and ourselves, with a new lens.

When we're not aware of our self-limiting beliefs and autopilot reactions, our negative relationship loops color how we see ourselves and others. We may point to others' behavior as the cause of our own actions. Or we may blame ourselves for how stupidly we act over and over again in the same situation. In any case, the result is blame. We either blame others or blame ourselves for our unproductive interactions and relationship struggles. All the while, we remain unaware that a negative loop, including our active role in perpetuating it, even exists.

Negative relationship loops are the behavioral manifestation of our visceral memories. What we say and do is influenced by our mindsets, which themselves are influenced by our big and little impacts, the messages from those impacts, the beliefs tied to those messages, and then the autopilot thoughts and behaviors that kick in as a result. If we're not aware of all that's driving us, we'll continue to experience—

and respond to—the world in the same old way. Over and over and over again. When other people join us in responding the same way all the time, we end up in a loop.

The book *Leadership and Self-Deception*[19] by the Arbinger Institute describes a social dynamic called "collusion" in which two people participate in a consistent pattern of interactions that reinforce negative views of each other and lead to less-than-desirable behavior between the two parties. It's a powerful concept that I've adapted to highlight how relationship loops work between individuals, teams, and groups.

In any given interaction, we experience others doing or saying something. Our perception of what they say or do goes through a natural filter that's colored by our impacts and the beliefs connected to those impacts. It's totally normal and logical to respond based on our filters. How we interpret what others say or do becomes objective truth to us. In my case, I really believed Drew wasn't pulling his weight. Based on how I defined the situation for myself, he truly wasn't. The problem was that I wasn't allowing myself to consider a broader view of our distinct contributions. As a result, my autopilot response was a shift in my tone of voice and the language I used, as well as an arrogant look on my face that expressed my disapproval.

Drew, on the other hand, was a peacemaker. He was great with clients and never confrontational, even with the most difficult people in the most challenging situations. I don't know what Drew thought as I responded to benign situations with judgmental scowls, but he rarely said a challenging word to me, which made it easy for me to continue my un-partner-like behavior.

Relationship loops work like this:

1. **My Experience:** My perception of the experience, influenced by my beliefs and feelings
2. **My Response:** My behavior, based on my thoughts, feelings, and autopilot responses
3. **Their Experience:** Others' perception of my responses, influenced by their own beliefs and feelings
4. **Their Response:** Others' behavior, based on their own thoughts, feelings, and autopilot responses

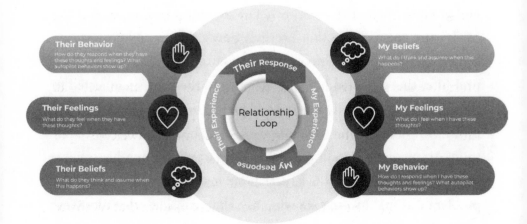

Relationship Loop | Relationship Loops Involve Cycles of Experiences and Responses

Relationship loops are the forces that shape the cultures of families, friendships, teams, and organizations. These relational patterns can be hard to see, and thus hard to break. The stronger and more dysfunctional the autopilot responses within the relationship loop, the more destructive they can get. Relationship loops may also be referred to as "feedback loops" or "collusion cycles." But whereas many models of loops or cycles focus on negative dynamics, relationship loops can also be positive. Positive relationship loops reinforce generative interactions, collaboration, and high-performing team and organizational cultures. The goal is to replace our negative relationship loops with positive ones and, in so doing, transform ourselves, our teams, and our organizations.

It's also possible to bring relationship loops with us into our daily interactions with total strangers. For example, if I hold a self-limiting belief that people are untrustworthy, I may approach my many interactions with a self-protectiveness that can taint my entire experience of the world. If I'm shopping in a store, and the clerk approaches me to see if I want any help, I might respond to their inquiry with a bit of standoffishness—a neutral rather than appreciative facial expression, a monotone voice rather than one that expresses gratitude, and curt language that minimizes the conversation. In response, the clerk may experience me as unwelcoming or unpleasant, so they may be less inclined to smile or engage in ways that would indicate they do care if I find what I'm looking for in the store. In this simple example, I impact others in ways that reinforce my self-limiting belief because my actions create a greater chance of experiencing a behavioral response that reinforces my belief (in this case, that people are untrustworthy). Wherever I go in life, I recreate my reality by reinforcing my negative relationship loop. I produce a present-day reality for myself that extends into the future by reenacting a relationship loop over and over.

Use the Relationship Loop Model to zero in on the dynamics of one of your current personal or professional relationships so you can understand the loops that may exist. Refer to your Autopilot Mapper to reference your impacts, messages, beliefs, and autopilots, and consider how they may be showing up and influencing your current relationships. Pick an experience that you see as either positive or negative for a given relationship. Answer the questions across each step of the loop: My Beliefs, My Feelings, My Behavior, Their Beliefs, Their Feelings, and Their Behavior. Of course, you may not know the other person or group's experience unless you have spoken to them directly about it. If not, just try to put yourself in their shoes and consider how they might experience your specific response, given what you know about your history together.

Negative relationship loops get reinforced and perpetuated over time, which is why at times we can feel "stuck" in our relationships. Exposing your relationship loops is an important step in growing your XQ. Because your mindsets and the way you apply your abilities are typically connected to relationships with other individuals or groups of people, gaining insight into the dynamics between ourselves and others can be enlightening. Examining our stagnant relationships with a new lens can give us newfound motivation to reinvent how we show up, the boundaries we hold, and our future expectations for the quality of our relationships.

CREATE POSITIVE LOOPS

As you explore your XQ, you will get a better sense of your deeper self and the things that make you tick. You may also recognize the specific self-limiting beliefs that no longer work for you, as well as the self-expanding beliefs you want to replace them with. As a result, you'll gain more clarity on what you want for your future. You may also recognize that certain relationships you have are in sync with your goals, while some are less so. You may discover a fresh motivation to reevaluate your current relationships or create new ones altogether.

Sometimes reinventing your relationship loops requires setting new boundaries for yourself and with others. You may need to start or stop doing things so you don't continue contributing to unproductive loops that reinforce your self-limiting beliefs. While it may disrupt the status quo of a relationship for a while, it's often better to sever or challenge a toxic relationship than to continue to live with the dysfunction it brings. In the work world, it can be quite difficult to set boundaries in the spirit of reinventing relationships with your manager, another team, or people in positions of authority. But as you embrace your XQ, you might recognize that you have more to gain than lose if you truly desire positive change in your personal or professional life.

So, how do you shift your relationship loops from negative to positive? Share your experience of developing your XQ, including any ideas about your existing relationship loops:

- With your family
- With friends
- With your team
- In your leadership development programs
- In your mentoring and coaching programs
- In other contexts that relate to your personal and professional goals

The objective is to obtain feedback on your perceptions of your relationship loops. This can be tricky, however, if there's defensiveness or any resentment at play due to self-limiting beliefs and autopilot reactions. But if you and others in your relationship loops approach things with curiosity, appreciation, and a desire to improve the relationship, amazing changes can result.

YOU, AMPLIFIED

Self-awareness, groundedness, or centeredness—whatever you call it, when you have it, you feel it. You remain present. You don't get riled up. You're not scared to get vulnerable to make yourself even more effective. You apply your self-expanding beliefs to lead yourself toward new endeavors. You tap into your abilities in new ways. Your demeanor and behavior become the standard for others around you. You become a role model. All this comes from the combination of XQ and EQ. It's hard to grow one without growing the other.

Developing yourself often involves positively impacting others in the process. That's why they say there's no better way to learn something than to teach it to someone else. Mutual growth and development are characteristic of many positive relationship loops. I call it *amplification*. Amplification is the process of growing XQ through positive relationship loops.

My beliefs surrounding my own relationships shifted as part of my own XQ development. I recognized the important role of vulnerability. I realized that being vulnerable didn't mean I was weak; in fact, it was the opposite. Being vulnerable required courage. Getting in touch with and sharing my struggles, pain, fears, and joy with other people, especially my male friends and colleagues, became an important facet of my relationships. I found that the more I disclosed, the more others disclosed about themselves to me. I shared things with close friends that I hadn't shared before about my childhood, personal struggles, self-limiting beliefs, and more. And they shared, too—not just with me, but also with each other. My proactive vulnerability created a safe space for more vulnerability, which deepened relationships I had thought were already deep.

I've done my best to demonstrate the power of developing XQ through my own story in this book. At times, I've felt hesitant to disclose such personal details of my life because many of my professional contacts will now read my harrowing stories. I don't know how they'll respond or what they'll say. That's what vulnerability is all about—choosing to expose ourselves to the potential judgment of others with the intention of creating deeper relational connections with those who will embrace us for all of who we are.

Amplification doesn't just happen between individuals. Teams, organizations, and even communities can also have impacts and hold self-limiting beliefs. The same approaches I've described in the previous chapters can be applied on a broader scale to teams and organizations. Groups of people working together on shared goals can demonstrate "collective XQ." When people have shared experiences due to specific events or because they're in the same organization day after day, the same dynamics are at play: they collectively obtain impacts, develop beliefs, and participate in relationship loops.

The best working environments are those where you bring your best while also bringing out the best in others. Amplification is how you do that. Anyone can decide to develop their XQ, amplify it, and create positive relationship loops that change the cultures of their teams and organizations. Leaders can model XQ and spread it through the ranks. Even more importantly, anyone can spread the benefits of XQ from anywhere within an organization by simply embracing it for themselves. This is how real change happens.

Every one of us is on our own personal journey, but many of us share similar self-limiting beliefs. As you gain experience in growing your own XQ, you can help others do the same. Imparting the wisdom gained from your own journey, either directly or through your example, can give others the encouragement to embark on their own processes. They, in turn, can eventually help others as well. And so on. It's you, amplified.

CHAPTER SEVEN KEY MESSAGES:

- The thoughts, feelings, and behaviors that automatically arise when you're triggered are your autopilot responses.
- The Autopilot Mapper template provides a tool to understand how your impacts, the messages from those impacts, and your self-limiting beliefs lead to your autopilots.
- Because beliefs and emotions are typically connected, developing your *Emotional* Intelligence can accelerate the growth of your *Experiential* Intelligence, which helps prevent unproductive autopilot responses in your relationships.
- Individual and group relationships can get stuck in debilitating patterns called negative relationship loops.
- By developing your Emotional and Experiential Intelligence, you can transform your unworkable relationships into positive relationship loops that advance personal goals, elevate team effectiveness, and strengthen team and organizational culture.

8

ASSESS XQ

Chapter Eight Video Overview

E ven if you don't believe much is currently getting in the way of your success, it's still worth evaluating your own Experiential Intelligence (XQ). Getting a sense of how you view your mindsets, abilities, and know-how can provide you with insights about yourself that you can use for self-improvement. That's what the XQ Snapshot does, by providing a qualitative picture of what you see as your most impactful experiences, mindsets, abilities, and know-how.

To measure your XQ quantitatively, I created the XQ Assessment in partnership with Lindsey Godwin, a professor of management and academic director of the David L. Cooperrider Center for Appreciative Inquiry at Champlain College. Many people, and especially busy people in business, just want a quick assessment to tell them how they're doing and where they might have work to do on themselves. If you like quick assessments that take less than three minutes to complete and give you a numeric score with a brief interpretation of your results, the XQ Assessment can give you a good baseline.

I've made the assessment freely available as part of a research project on measuring Experiential Intelligence. You can take the assessment and get your score at https://sorenkaplan.com/XQAssessment.

Use the QR Code to Take the XQ Assessment

The remainder of this chapter outlines the structure of the assessment and a detailed description of what it measures. If you want to assess your XQ without being influenced by this information, take the assessment first and then return to this chapter.

THE XQ ASSESSMENT SCALE

In order to measure progress over time, it's helpful to measure concepts like XQ as much as possible. This is true at the individual level, but especially for teams and organizations driven by performance metrics.

The XQ Assessment Scale consists of twelve statements within four categories: Ability Appreciation, Impact Awareness, Mindset Flexibility, and Amplification.

- **Ability Appreciation** is your recognition that you possess specific strengths in the form of attitudes, assumptions, knowledge, or skills due to your unique experiences.
- **Impact Awareness** is your attunement to the impacts you've experienced in life and how to view and use them to your advantage.
- **Mindset Flexibility** is your awareness that your attitudes and beliefs will change over time based on your experiences.
- **Amplification** involves sharing your XQ journey while providing a safe, trusted space for others to openly share and receive your insight and encouragement at the same time.

There are three statements within each of these categories that, collectively, can help you understand your XQ. The three statements in each category emphasize the past, present, and future, and responses to these statements are recorded on a *Strongly Agree* to *Strongly Disagree* scale. The statements are as follows:

Ability Appreciation

1. I developed unique skills and abilities from the life experiences I had growing up.
2. I frequently use abilities and skills that I developed outside of

any formal education or training to accomplish things in my life.

3. My unique skills and abilities are a solid foundation for what I want to achieve in the future.

Impact Awareness

1. I have reflected on both the positive and negative experiences from my past to learn from them.

2. I understand how my past experiences inform my actions in the present.

3. Even my most painful experiences have taught me valuable lessons that will help me be successful in the future.

Mindset Flexibility

1. Looking back across my past, I held attitudes and beliefs that I now realize aren't actually true.

2. I am able to shift my thinking when I recognize that certain attitudes and beliefs I hold are getting in my way.

3. I fully expect that some of the attitudes and beliefs I hold today will change in the future.

Amplification

1. I have openly shared stories about both my past successes and personal struggles with people I trust.

2. I value being a trusted person with whom others can share their successes and struggles.

3. I can imagine sharing my personal experiences with others in the future to help them grow.

The statements within each category are intentionally designed to have a past, present, and future focus. The first statement addresses behaviors and attitudes about the past, including either how respondents view the past or have productively worked with their past experiences. The next statement addresses the present and how respondents relate to their current experiences. The third statement focuses on how ready and able respondents are to proactively move toward their desired futures.

Focus	Past — Appreciation of the Past	Present — Connection to the Present	Future — Focus on the Future
Ability Appreciation	• I developed unique skills and abilities from the life experiences I had growing up.	• I frequently use abilities and skills that I developed outside of any formal education or training to accomplish things in my life.	• My unique skills and abilities are a solid foundation for what I want to achieve in the future.
Impact Awareness	• I have reflected on both the positive and negative experiences from my past to learn from them.	• I understand how my past experiences inform my actions in the present.	• Even my most painful experiences have taught me valuable lessons that will help me be successful in the future.
Mindset Flexibility	• Looking back across my past, I held attitudes and beliefs that I now realize aren't actually true.	• I am able to shift my thinking when I recognize that certain attitudes and beliefs I hold are getting in my way.	• I fully expect that some of the attitudes and beliefs I hold today will change in the future.
Amplification	• I have openly shared stories about both my past successes and personal struggles with people I trust.	• I value being a trusted person with whom others can share their successes and struggles.	• I can imagine sharing my personal experiences with others in the future to help them grow.

XQ Assessment Scale

Look Across the Past, Present, and Future to Measure XQ

By assigning a score ranging from 1 to 5 to your answers, with one point given to answers of "Strongly Disagree" and five points to answers of "Strongly Agree," it's possible to calculate scores for each XQ category using this scale:

1 = Strongly Disagree
2 = Disagree

3 = Somewhat Agree

4 = Agree

5 = Strongly Agree

Given that there are twelve statements, scores for the assessment can range from a low of 12 to a high of 60. Calculate your overall score to determine where you fall on the scale. I've created three levels of XQ based on the total score to help categorize results into a unique persona: Aspirant, Explorer, and Amplifier.

Score	Your XQ Level	Description
49-60	Amplifier	As an Amplifier, you're ready to take your high XQ and contribute your know-how in developing XQ with others.
37-48	Explorer	As an Explorer, you've recognized that your past can weigh you down if you let it, and your biggest opportunity now is to further explore the positive and negative impacts of your past to see what beliefs they shaped.
12-36	Aspirant	As an Aspirant, you're ready to grow your XQ. It's possible you may be anchored in the past and being held back by certain mindsets that are getting in your way of progress.

XQ Assessment Profiles

Three Profiles Correspond to Three Levels of XQ

A score between 12 and 36 means you're an Aspirant and ready to grow your XQ. A score of 37 through 48 means you're an Explorer and well on your way to achieving high XQ. A score of 49 or above means you're an Amplifier and ready to expand your XQ through helping others further develop their own XQ.

The Aspirant

As an Aspirant, you're ready to grow your XQ. It's quite possible that you are anchored in the past and held back by certain mindsets getting in your way of progress. Taking an honest look at the experiences that have shaped you, even the difficult ones, may help you see your current situation and strengths in a new light. Continue reading, talking to others about XQ, and using the various tools and templates in this book. Because your past might be challenging to explore, especially if you've experienced a trauma, it can be helpful to get support from a person you trust, like a professional coach, mentor, advisor, therapist, or someone else. Take the XQ Assessment again in a few months to check in on your progress. Keep at it. Growing your Experience Intelligence can take time, but it's well worth it.

The Explorer

As an Explorer, you're well on your way to achieving high XQ. You recognize that your past can weigh you down if you let it. You've already taken an introspective look at the impacts of your experiences to ensure that you continue moving forward in a positive way. You realize that your attitudes and beliefs may change over time as you gain new insight into yourself, your relationships, and the world. Discovering and using your strengths are already important to you. While you possess this insight into your abilities, however, you know there's still more to learn and find and that there are more positive changes ahead. Your biggest opportunity now is to further explore your current mindsets through looking at both the positive and negative impacts of your past to see what beliefs they shaped. You can also create new experiences for yourself that are focused on the abilities you want to develop. Sharing your goals, thinking, and feelings with someone you trust can help accelerate the process of exploring and growing your XQ.

The Amplifier

As an Amplifier, you're ready to take your high Experiential Intelligence and contribute to helping others develop their own XQ. You recognize that as you develop greater self-awareness, it's natural to leave old mindsets behind. You value looking inward. Your biggest opportunity, as well as contribution, lies in role-modeling vulnerability to create a safe space where others feel comfortable sharing their own stories. Because you've already learned so much about your mindsets, abilities, and know-how from your experiences, you can teach others to consider how the events of their own lives have instilled strengths they can use in positive ways. Supporting others who have an interest in growing their XQ will help you continue developing your own at the same time.

Moving from Numbers to Insight

In today's world of artificial intelligence, big data, blockchains, and dashboards, it's tempting to reduce our intelligence to a number. We've done that for years with the Intelligence Quotient (IQ). And there are now dozens of surveys and questionnaires that promise to assess Emotional Intelligence (EQ). While the XQ Snapshot and Assessment Scale can be useful starting points for understanding your Experiential Intelligence, they're not the end goal.

The most valuable part of the XQ Assessment is the follow-up work you do by reflecting on your results yourself or discussing them with others you trust. It's easy to select "Strongly Agree" as a response to all the statements. It's a lot harder to vulnerably share the examples, stories, and experiences that the statements address. For example, the third statement in the Impact Awareness category, "Even my most painful experiences have taught me valuable lessons that will help me be successful in the future," has a follow-up question: *What were those experiences, and what did you learn from them that you're consciously using today to achieve your goals?* Also consider the Mindset Flexibility statement "I am able to shift my thinking when I recognize that certain attitudes and beliefs I hold are getting in my way," which naturally leads to the question: *What attitudes and beliefs do you think you hold, and why would they be getting in the way?* Or, in the Ability Appreciation category, the statement "I developed unique skills and abilities from the life experiences I had growing up" also asks, *What unique skills and abilities* did *you develop, and which experiences did they result from?* And finally, when it comes to Amplification, the statement "I can imagine sharing my personal experiences with others in the future to help them grow" begs a simple question: *Why?*

In fact, if you deeply reflect upon these follow-up questions, it's possible you might think you "overscored" yourself on the assessment. If you've already taken the assessment, think about the specifics underlying each statement. Would you change your original responses if you were asked to share answers vulnerably and honestly to these follow-up questions? If you haven't yet taken the assessment, consider what's underneath the statements at a much deeper level before you "Strongly Agree" with them.

The same goes for the XQ Snapshot. It may be easy to churn out a surface-level response. Getting to your most meaningful answers, however, may take some introspection. Vulnerably discussing your answers with others undoubtedly will.

ASSESSING COLLECTIVE XQ FOR TEAMS AND ORGANIZATIONS

If you're part of a team or working in an organization, you may want to assess the collective XQ of your group. There are three ways to go about doing this:

1. Each team member takes the individual assessment, and then the group discusses the individual results
2. Each team member takes the individual assessment, and then the group discusses the aggregated, collective scores
3. A combination of the above

To get the most out of the assessment, it can be helpful first to lead a group discussion that provides context for what XQ is and why developing it for your team is important. Have your team complete the assessment, and then explore individual findings and their implications for your team or organization. It's valuable to discuss the reasons and rationale underlying how people answered certain questions. It may also be valuable to create your own version of the assessment by modifying the statements to reflect the unique language or terminology used in your organization.

FUTURE DIRECTIONS FOR RESEARCHERS AND PROFESSIONALS

The XQ Assessment in this book provides a structured way to gather data about people's self-perceptions of their Experiential Intelligence. The assessment is just one starting point for understanding XQ. There are many other dimensions worthy of exploring qualitatively and quantitatively to help assess, develop, and amplify Experiential Intelligence. Questions to consider as guideposts for future research include:

- How do we most effectively measure our self-awareness of our mindsets, including our attitudes and beliefs about ourselves, others, and the world?
- How do certain mindsets and abilities lead to greater personal and professional success?
- What are the mechanisms by which humility leads to self-awareness?
- What are the mechanisms by which demonstrating humility and vulnerability can lead to greater humility and vulnerability in others?
- How can two people experience the same thing, especially a trauma, yet have completely different long-term impacts from the experience?
- How does IQ correlate with XQ?

- How does EQ correlate with XQ?
- In what ways is XQ a cross-cultural concept, and in what ways does it differ across cultures?

For those interested in further researching Experiential Intelligence, I encourage you to combine multiple approaches. It's usually by connecting top-down hypothesis testing with bottom-up qualitative research that the greatest insight is achieved.

Let's shift gears now and look at how to apply XQ to your own leadership, as well as to the teams, organizations, and communities to which you belong.

CHAPTER EIGHT KEY MESSAGES:

- XQ can be assessed qualitatively and quantitatively for individuals, teams, and organizations.
- Take the XQ assessment and get your score at https://soren kaplan.com/XQAssessment.
- The XQ Assessment includes twelve statements across four categories: Ability Appreciation, Impact Awareness, Mindset Flexibility, and Amplification.
- Many opportunities exist for additional research into XQ as a concept and methodology.

Part Three
APPLY XQ

9

LEADERSHIP XQ

Chapter Nine Video Overview

The task of leadership is to create an alignment of strengths in ways that make the system's weaknesses irrelevant,"[20] said Peter Drucker, the iconic management expert.

When it comes to Experiential Intelligence (XQ), Drucker's summary of the essence of leadership rings true: you need to discover and use your collective strengths as a leader in order to effectively elicit and align the aggregate strengths of your followers to drive breakthrough innovation or transform your organization.

As a leader, you'll be way more effective if you're deliberate about what you draw upon from on your experiences. Gaining insight into your self-limiting beliefs and autopilot responses allows you to avoid being steered by them, while making it easier for your strengths to rise to the surface. Leveraging your XQ positions you to better navigate tough situations and avoid making poor decisions. And because leadership itself is a social relationship between a leader and their followers, your ability to role-model high XQ can have a significant impact on how others show up and support collective, positive change.

With self-awareness typically comes greater intentionality in what you do and how you relate as a leader. Just because you manage people doesn't mean you're actually leading them. They might do what you say because you're the boss, but that's not leadership. Knowing why you do what you do often leads to a desire to do something meaningful and build purposeful relationships. As you move forward with intention, your behavior will influence others, who will then be inspired to follow you because of your vision for the future combined with the promise of achieving meaningful goals. But even more important will be your mutually beneficial relationship that draws upon your assets while simultaneously drawing out your team's own strengths and motivation—which will catalyze their contribution to the cause. That's leadership.

As you see your impact on others, you'll gain greater insight into yourself as a leader and in relationship to your followers. It's a cycle. When you drive this cycle forward by tapping into your Emotional Intelligence (EQ) and XQ, helping others tap into these for themselves, you're better positioned to lead transformative change and breakthroughs.

Becoming a leader doesn't happen overnight. It takes time and, usually, a lot of experiences—both positive and challenging—that build the mindsets, abilities, and know-how that'll set you up for what's next. In 2001, for example, a few months prior to the infamous dot-com crash, I left my job running the strategy consulting group at HP. For five years prior to my departure, I had observed the explosive growth of a new generation of software companies around me in Silicon Valley, including Yahoo and Google. I wanted the status and glory of being a founder myself, not to mention the title of CEO and potentially hitting a big pay day by taking a company public. So I departed from HP and founded a software company focused on providing a platform for creating "online communities." I believed there was a big opportunity for helping organizations arrange networks of people using web-based tools. In many ways, it was a precursor to what LinkedIn and Meta (formerly Facebook) call their "groups" today.

A few months after trading in my stable corporate job for the unpredictable start-up life, my second daughter was born. It was a joyous occasion that added to my overall conviction that my decision to launch a start-up was a good one and would lead to a new chapter of growth—for our family, my career, and me personally.

That exhilarating feeling lasted exactly four days. September 11, 2001, shocked the world when the World Trade Center towers in New York collapsed after an unprecedented terrorist attack. The stock market tanked. The economy froze. Everyone stopped buying software.

When the world ground to a halt, so did our company. To make matters worse, we didn't have funding, so there was no budget for marketing. We reduced people's pay to below-market wages with the promise that, when things got better, so would their salaries. I expected the downturn to end, but I had no idea when that would be. My response to this dire situation would turn out to include some of the worst decisions of my career and would lead to my departure from the company I founded.

So, what did I do in the midst of the crisis? I focused all of my efforts on trying to champion the idea that "online communities" were the wave of the future. I wrote lots of articles and posted on our blog. While we got a bit of press, we didn't get many customers. That's because I lost sight of what problems I should have been helping customers address, especially in the tumultuous economic times of the early 2000s. People just didn't know what "online communities" were back then or why they would need them. I had also created a big vision for our software platform, one that included basically every feature under the sun: live video, online discussions, calendaring, document management, web-based learning tools, and more. It was a hodgepodge of features without focus. The approach I led the company to take was the exact opposite of what we know as agile software development today.

In retrospect, the fundamental reason I founded the start-up in the first place had to do with my desire to show the world—and myself—that I was capable and worthy of attention. These were the same things I had longed to be while growing up, and the self-limiting belief I'd developed by then was that I was neither. So, instead of creating a company focused on solving meaningful problems and making the biggest contribution to the world as possible, my primary motivation was driven by the subconscious desire to overcome my self-limiting belief. This led me to make a cascade of poor decisions without realizing it. Just like how I hunkered down as a kid and became incredibly self-sufficient due to my circumstances, I reverted to another self-limiting belief: that, in order to get through tough times, I needed to step up and go it alone. Instead of engaging the team in debating the challenges in front of us, I sat in my office debating myself in my head.

The street smarts I'd developed early on ended up outsmarting me as I retreated into my own little world of trying to make things work.

I floundered around for a few years without moving the needle. Our small team of about fifteen employees included many skilled, well-intentioned people, yet I felt alone much of the time as I defined our strategy, struggled to drum up sales, figured out the next product features to develop, and ensured the few customers we had would stay around long enough to renew their licenses. The financial realities of the business, combined with my dwindling savings and the need to support my family, forced me to move on. I definitely didn't succeed in the traditional sense of the word. Yet, without knowing it at the time, these experiences shaped my mindsets, abilities, and know-how in ways that have become some of my greatest strengths, which I have applied successfully in other business ventures.

After I stepped down from my start-up, I decided to go back to what I knew best: consulting teams to help them collaboratively define their business strategies and plans. It felt a bit ironic that I had just failed in my own business and was now helping others figure out strategies for theirs. But I knew that I was adept at seeing trends, identifying market opportunities, and facilitating thorny discussions to help teams find common ground. Plus, I also recognized that it's one thing to serve as an objective third party to help others, but a very different thing to apply the same strategies to oneself. That's why people need consultants in the first place—they're often too close to their issues to see them clearly, and their mindsets inevitably get in the way. The question for me now was how I would find clients who would want my consulting.

In my start-up, because we didn't have money for marketing, I wrote lots of articles, published them on our website, and optimized our web pages for keywords related to our software. I had essentially been doing "content marketing" before it was a common term. So I did the same thing with my new consulting website. Within a few short months, the site rose to the top of Google's search results, so that anyone looking for "innovation consulting" would discover my website. I partnered up with a colleague to help run our business and hired a few subcontractors. We obtained clients like Disney, Colgate-Palmolive, Visa, Medtronic, and the American Nurses Association, all of whom discovered our firm after simple internet searches. The abilities I had acquired from using scrappy marketing tactics from my failed start-up led to a thriving consulting business.

About a decade into my new consulting career, I met a neighbor named Michael Lynch down the street at a barbeque. Michael had been CEO of a company and had just sold it to software giant SAP, where he remained as a head of their "Internet of Things" business. An entrepreneur at heart, Michael wanted to leave corporate life. So we found a few consulting projects that he could work on with me while he explored his future options.

One day, Michael asked me a perplexing question: "How do we scale what you know?"

"What do you mean?" I asked.

"You've seen how so many companies operate, what makes teams effective, and the business processes that give organizations the edge when it comes to innovation. How do we get that out of your head and provide it to the world as a business?"

"What do you mean?" I asked again.

Michael basically gave me the same impassioned pitch he had used on venture capitalists to secure millions in funding for his prior company. "We can take what you know how to do with all these companies and turn it into a software platform. And you can get other experts like yourself to contribute the wisdom from their own vast experience. Anyone can then find and apply expertise from the world's experts instantly for themselves, with their teams, and for their organization. It would be like having you and an army of seasoned consultants in your pocket."

I was sold.

I was also sold on the fact that I would need to apply what I'd learned from my experiences with my first start-up—both in terms of what to do and, especially, what not to do—in this new venture. Michael and I compared what we had learned from our business experiences as we formulated our strategy. But we went much deeper than that.

Michael and I both had tough childhoods. We each excelled in many ways professionally despite less than ideal upbringings. We recognized that we carried around impacts from our past that could get in our way, both personally and professionally. We discussed it all. We gained insight into ourselves, each other, and especially how our self-limiting beliefs and autopilot responses show up when we're dealing with uncertainty and stress. We identified the mindsets, abilities, and know-how we each brought to the new venture. We also recognized that we needed to bring in others with complementary experiences to join our team, which has become a true success factor in what we do, and which I'll describe in more detail in the next chapter.

My story here isn't about perfect leadership. My journey has been punctuated with starts, stops, successes, and failures. But one thread ties all of my leadership strands together: my belief that every one of my experiences has built upon the last and will become a foundation for the next. By connecting the dots across my experiences, I've been able to identify my barriers and uncover my success factors. I've taken my own personal insights and connected them to what I've consistently seen in leaders who embrace their broader experiences as part of who they are and how they lead. From all this, I've identified five important strategies for leading in today's disruptive world that leverage and grow Experiential Intelligence.

LEADERSHIP STRATEGY #1: CONNECT DOTS TO FIND FOCUS

This first strategy is perfectly illustrated by the story of when Steve Jobs dropped out of college and serendipitously stumbled upon a calligraphy course advertised on a bulletin board. Intrigued by the design of the flyer, he audited the class, even though he wasn't a student at the college anymore. The experience stuck with him when he went back to Silicon Valley, and he eventually connected what he learned in the course to the design of the Apple Macintosh, creating an operating system with a user interface based on various "fonts." Steve Jobs connected the dots of his experiences to deliver a game-changing innovation and a game-changing company: Apple. That's often what distinguishes innovators. They make connections that others don't see and then reveal those connections to the world through doing something novel.

I've seen many executives embark on a new job or business venture and fail to fully draw upon their prior experiences when doing so. They fail to fully appreciate that the strengths they developed over time in both their personal and professional lives are just waiting to be leveraged in the new opportunity. They don't take the time to pause, look back, and recognize the myriad connections and experiences that got them to where they are. The collective assets they possess that allowed them to arrive at that particular position, at that specific organization, in that exact moment of time, don't exist accidentally. All of their experiences, from childhood to present day, contributed to their success—and a great opportunity remains to tap into the strengths instilled by them to take things to the next level.

I've tried my best to embody this concept myself in my role at my latest venture, Praxie.com. I've applied what I've learned about myself from my challenging childhood, my experience with my failed start-up, and the abilities and know-how gained from my consulting and leadership development work. As I help build a company that allows anyone, anywhere, to benefit from the vast Experiential Intelligence that exists in the world at an affordable price, my dots have come together to provide my focus and the means to bring it to life.

We all have dots. But we don't always connect them. And that's where the opportunity lies for you as a leader.

Connect your dots to find your focus.

LEADERSHIP STRATEGY #2: REWRITE THE UNWRITTEN RULES

Many books, articles, and speakers advocate breaking rules, challenging them, and rewriting them. We've seen entire industries upended when companies with new business models overcome the presumed rules held by the competition. Netflix did this with streaming entertainment. Southwest did this with its low-cost airline. Amazon did this with e-commerce. Tesla did this with the electric car. Leaders challenge existing rules and then replace them with better ones.

A great starting point in developing your leadership capacity is your own attitudes and beliefs. Attitudes and beliefs make up your mindsets. They're essentially your unwritten rules, and we all have them. The same dynamic of unquestioned attitudes and beliefs exists at a broader level, when the leaders of the vast majority of organizations in an industry all hold the same unwritten rules—which is why entire industries can be upended by a single company that introduces a breakthrough product or builds an innovative new business model. The goal, then, is to develop greater awareness of the unwritten rules you hold because of the markets you serve or the broader business you're in. To lead your industry, you need to challenge your prevailing attitudes and beliefs. When you become aware of your mindsets, the unwritten rules that you've been following will give way to new possibilities. You get to rewrite the rules for yourself as a leader, your organization, and even your industry.

In the case of Praxie, we're challenging the unwritten rule that the mindsets, abilities, and know-how from people's lifelong experiences are lost when they stop working or leave an organization. Underlying this unwritten rule is the prevailing self-limiting belief that such intangible experience cannot easily be codified and scaled up in ways that give less experienced people the ability to do the same things as the experts. For example, an entire industry exists that provides specific software applications for creating business strategies, running business processes, and managing projects. Many of these systems have indeed been built by domain experts. But the problem is that the world changes quickly, so the "hard-coded" tools they've created, even when promoted as customizable, aren't actually very flexible. What's needed are simple tools that anyone, even those without technical knowledge, can use to take the knowledge in their heads and that resides in their teams, and instantly digitize it into a simple sequence of steps. The burgeoning field of "no-code" software is challenging the entire software industry itself, and our team at Praxie is helping to lead the way.

Rewrite your own unwritten rules to rewrite the rules for your industry.

LEADERSHIP STRATEGY #3: EXPLORE UNCERTAINTY TO DISCOVER NEW OPPORTUNITIES

Given my early childhood experiences, I became adept at navigating ambiguous situations and trusting they would turn out okay. So I was fortunate to be able to draw upon a self-expanding belief as I founded my first start-up, built my consulting and leadership development business, and then started Praxie: *within uncertainty lies opportunity.*

It's not always easy to start doing something when uncertainty is staring you in the face. Many people experience fear when faced with the unknown. It's natural to feel anxious when what might happen next is highly uncertain. The problem is that fear can be paralyzing. And what's really needed in ambiguous situations is agility. Fritz Perls, the psychotherapist who developed Gestalt therapy, once said, "Fear is excitement without the breath."[21] Fear gets in the way of a lot of things, from business innovation to making choices that can change one's personal life.

As a leader, if you accept that you may feel fear, and sit with it without self-judgment, you'll more effectively move through it to find the excitement on the other side. When you learn to do this for yourself, you'll become better equipped to help others do it for themselves as you lead them into an inherently uncertain future focused on new opportunities.

New business opportunities typically include an element of uncertainty. I'm not saying you need to take undue risks. But when you're presented with something that prompts you to face the unknown—whether it's taking on a new project, moving to a new job, or deciding to take some time off—remember that it can be an opportunity to tap into and grow your XQ. Better yet, a bigger opportunity involves proactively seeking out uncertainty. In business, innovation requires doing something new; otherwise, by definition, it's not innovative. Create a new product, service, or entirely new business. Challenge your industry's assumptions and business models. The outcomes of these actions are inherently uncertain. But if you don't do them, someone else will.

Explore uncertainty by embracing new experiences.

LEADERSHIP STRATEGY #4: CREATE EXPERIENCES TO SPARK POSITIVE CHANGE

As we've covered, the basis of XQ is that the experiences we have in life shape our mindsets, abilities, and know-how. Sometimes these experiences negatively impact us, which requires us to overcome their stifling effects. We've already discussed how these negative experiences, the ones that feel like an albatross hanging on our necks as we go about our lives, can nevertheless hold hidden strengths that you can draw upon for your leadership. Decoding these negative experiences often takes a significant effort. The positive experiences, on the other hand, tend to be more readily accessible. That's why, if you're a parent, you might consider what really gave you joy and excitement as a kid yourself, and then try to give those same experiences to your own child to help them grow, develop values, and appreciate life. It's not much different when it comes to harnessing the power of experience in your leadership.

Leadership, by its very nature, is social. It's impossible to lead when you have no one to rally behind your cause or for you to serve in some way. As a leader, you're influential. People listen and watch, and then make meaning from what they hear and see. So you have an opportunity to consciously create experiences for others that convey and instill useful mindsets, abilities, and know-how focused on what you're trying to achieve. A speech is an experience. An awards ceremony is an experience. Creating a new product is an experience. A social protest is an experience. It's not rocket science, but it takes intention and effort to consciously create these kinds of experiences, especially when fighting the fires of running a business.

I've already described how organizational culture is created. People have experiences. Their experiences create assumptions. Their assumptions shape behavior. It's your job to be conscious of the experiences people have as a result of what you do. You also need to be sensitive to how their responses impact you as part of the overall leader-follower relationship. If you're not, you may create experiences that inadvertently reinforce mindsets that run counter to your intentions and the things you want to achieve. You can generate experiences that promote innovation or that stifle it. If you celebrate people who take risks, you'll get more innovation. If you fire them for failing, you'll signal to others it's not worth sticking their necks out to improve things. If you role-model the vulnerability involved in amplifying Experiential Intelligence, you'll see more of it in return.

Sometimes creating an experience is not about what you do or say, but about providing an immersion into something new and different. For example, I have led leadership development programs where entire executive teams travel to Silicon Valley for several days. While I could visit these teams back in their corporate offices, share case studies using beautiful presentations, and have discussions about the inner workings of Silicon Valley's culture, it wouldn't have the same effect. Visiting companies like Netflix, experiencing the innovation process at Stanford University's design school, touring start-up incubators like the Plug and Play Tech Center, and just getting immersed inside the energetic environment of Silicon Valley creates a visceral experience. It changes mindsets.

Consciously create experiences to craft culture and spark positive change.

LEADERSHIP STRATEGY #5: AMPLIFY STRENGTHS TO AMPLIFY IMPACT

A fundamental premise of Experiential Intelligence is that everyone has strengths. The goal isn't to ignore weaknesses but rather to examine them and possibly find a hidden strength embedded in what might be a perceived gap. A shift in understanding and attitude can mean a shift in possibilities. XQ assumes that all individuals possess strengths but that their past experiences may create self-limiting beliefs and autopilot responses that stifle their ability to achieve their highest potential level of performance or see new possibilities that drive innovation. Rather than operate by leveraging complementary strengths, negative relationship loops within a team and between teams can produce experiences that stifle collaboration, let alone breakthroughs. The strengths that reside within people and across teams can either be surfaced and leveraged or left untapped based on how leadership guides the culture.

Like Peter Drucker says, your most important job as a leader is to surface and amplify strengths within people, across teams, and for the organization itself. Don't underestimate your influence. Amplifying strengths involves drawing the inherent assets—mindsets, abilities, and know-how—out of every person, team, department, function, business unit, business partner, supplier, and community in which you operate. It means helping others reconcile their historical struggles so that they're not limited by them. It means demonstrating and role-modeling your experience with developing your own XQ. It may mean creating training programs and rethinking how your company evaluates performance. It may mean reshaping your culture to replace negative relationship loops with positive ones that fully leverage the collective strengths of the organization to deliver the most valuable and meaningful products and services possible.

Amplify strengths to amplify impact.

LEADERSHIP ABILITIES IN TODAY'S DISRUPTIVE WORLD

Even though the five abilities I described use their own unique language, they are very much connected to tried-and-true leadership strategies:

- *Connecting dots to find focus* is also about clearly defining your purpose, mission, vision, and values.
- *Rewriting the unwritten rules* is also about thinking like an industry disruptor and business model innovator.
- *Exploring uncertainty to discover new opportunities* also involves navigating the VUCA (Volatile, Uncertain, Complex, and Ambiguous) world we live in today while continuing to innovate the products, services, and customer experiences needed for the future.
- *Creating experiences to spark positive change* also includes the strategies and actions needed to shape organizational culture, one of leadership's most important imperatives.
- *Amplifying strengths to amplify impact* is exactly that—helping individuals, teams, and the organization see, understand, and grow from the inside out so that your organization can have an even greater positive impact in the world.

The five leadership abilities connect to attitudes and beliefs that, when embraced, will embolden you to expand your possibilities and elevate your impact. And, as a result, you will serve as a role model for others.

Grow these abilities and apply them to your team and in your organization. You'll grow everyone's XQ, which will grow your business in the process.

CHAPTER NINE KEY MESSAGES:

- Leadership XQ involves synthesizing your own strengths as a leader to elicit the collective strengths of others.
- Five leadership strategies can help grow XQ for yourself, your team, and your organization, which in turn will grow your business. The five strategies include:
  - Connect dots to find focus
  - Rewrite the unwritten rules
  - Explore uncertainty to discover new opportunities
  - Create experiences to spark positive change
  - Amplify strengths to amplify impact

10

TEAM XQ

Chapter Ten Video Overview

There's no "I" in "team."

This pithy saying suggests that people need to give up their own agendas in the spirit of teamwork. Individual egos must take the back seat in service of the team's goals, since it's only the greater good of the team that matters. In theory, it makes sense. In practice, it's not realistic and even undermines what's most important for building a great team.

If you want breakthrough performance and innovation, you need to embrace the numerous "I's" on your team. In fact, you have as many "I's" as you have team members. Knowing that each team member is distinct will be a key success factor. It's essential to recognize and leverage differences that exist and to tap into what every person can uniquely contribute. Differences are what differentiate the best teams.

Team XQ is the collection of complementary mindsets, abilities, and know-how that empowers your team to achieve its goals. Teams are simply groups of people—people who bring their collective experiences, along with the impacts from those experiences and the associated mindsets, abilities, and know-how gained from them. How teams leverage the XQ of their individual members, the relationships that exist between team members, and the relationship loops that are created and recreated over time all influence the team's success.

There's lots of research and entire books on how to build and manage teams. I won't go into all the detail here. But having led my own teams, consulted with teams, and advised leaders on how to build teams, I've distilled what's most important for taking your team to the next level into three specific design principles. Consider these design principles as guideposts for what you can do to facilitate the types of relationships that lead to high performance and breakthrough innovation. These principles are also grounded in what's needed to both tap into the Experiential Intelligence (XQ) of your team and amplify it further.

STACK YOUR TEAM WITH DIVERSE EXPERIENCES

When we built our team at Praxie, we wanted to ensure our group possessed truly complementary experiences, both at the individual level and overall as a team. This meant we wanted people on the team who each possessed a diverse set of experiences. We also wanted our team as a whole to have synergistic mindsets, abilities, and know-how. Michael Lynch, as you may recall from earlier, had a successful company that he eventually sold to SAP. But Michael isn't just a software executive. He studied opera and had a starring role in the Broadway musical *Les Misérables* prior to getting into technology. The combination of his artistic background and business savvy makes him an amazing CEO. And then there's Michael Rothrock, another cofounder of Praxie and our Chief Technology Officer. Rothrock lives and breathes "agile," ensuring we apply both an agile mindset and practical tools to everything we do. It was the lack of an agile approach that was my biggest downfall in my previous start-up. Now we have someone who inspires us to continually challenge our assumptions, test ideas, and iterate quickly to find solutions and remain agile in everything we do. Gabriel Mendoza, who I met while at HP and working in Guadalajara, Mexico, brings extensive experience running digital businesses from his prior work at eBay and Intuit. Gabriel's cross-cultural experience gives him a unique ability to consider different perspectives when solving problems, empathize with a wide range of customers, and translate his insights into product requirements for our software.

And then there's Eyal Bloom. As a twenty-four-year-old, Eyal had almost zero business experience when she approached me for a job. Most companies would likely look at her résumé—if she even made it that far in the hiring process—and discard it without a blink. However, Eyal spent three years in the Israeli military and in her last year ended up as a commander overseeing a twenty-person battalion. When I met Eyal, I *knew* she would be a perfect fit. Nothing on her résumé said she had the ability to lead remote project teams with members in the United

States, India, and Africa. Nothing in her accomplishments signaled she knew how to build software applications focused on best-practice business processes. But, of course, she has done just that. It wasn't my intuition that told me she would be able to do all this. It was clear to me from her experience moving to Israel after middle school and being forced to adapt to a new culture, the discipline she would have needed to lead a military unit, and how she communicated her desire to learn and contribute that she would be an amazing complement to our team. For example, when I asked how she learned to lead her battalion, she replied, "I had to figure it out," which told me she was a clear problem-solver in even the most challenging social contexts. Eyal is a brilliant example of how Experiential Intelligence can be used across different contexts to excel, despite what appears as glaring holes on a résumé. From Eyal's fearlessness in taking on new challenges to her ability to coordinate a distributed team, she possesses mindsets, abilities, and know-how gleaned from experiences completely outside of business that still give her what's needed to succeed.

Some researchers use the term "cognitive diversity"[22] to describe how diverse thinking leads to better group problem-solving. Diversity in its broadest sense, beyond just cognition, is a success factor for most teams. And stacking your team with diverse *experiences* can lead to greater performance and innovation. Consider how life experiences, as well as business experiences and their resulting mindsets, abilities, and know-how, show up for individuals—and for the team itself. The trick is to create space for everyone to understand what everyone else can contribute on multiple dimensions. When you gain a greater appreciation for the ingredients everyone possesses, the cookbook of possibilities expands dramatically.

FOSTER POSITIVE RELATIONSHIP LOOPS

When you stack a team with diverse experiences that everyone understands and leverages, it sets the stage for creating positive relationship loops. When people on your team understand themselves better—the XQ they possess—they can more effectively articulate what they bring to the party. Other team members can then see the smorgasbord of assets that exist across the team and draw upon them as part of their daily work.

As a team leader, the way to facilitate positive relationship loops isn't necessarily to design specific work roles and processes that tap into people's assets. You can indeed do that. A more sustainable and scalable approach, and one that allows your team to move faster with agility, however, is to simply ensure that everyone understands the XQ that exists across the team.

At Praxie, for example, we understand that Michael Lynch possesses a strategic view of the market coupled with an uncanny ability to find creative solutions in the most challenging situations. We know that Michael Rothrock sees hidden assumptions, including how to test them quickly and effectively. We recognize that Gabriel can both immediately see the big picture as well as zero in on very specific actions to enhance customer experience. We draw upon Eyal to divvy up and manage our projects across our global team of subcontractors to leverage everyone's strengths. And the team knows that I'm able to articulate and communicate complex ideas in plain language so that our team, partners, and customers can easily understand what needs to be done and why. We complement each other and have created both formal and informal processes to draw upon. We apply what each and every one of us does best in a very organic way.

Positive relationship loops are created within teams when you minimize internal competition. Taking a lesson from physics, two objects can't occupy the same space at the same time. It's similar within and between teams. When people know that they complement each other, they don't try to invade each other's space or get ruffled by overlapping roles and agendas. When people are recognized and appreciated for what they bring to the party, they're more prone to discovering others' complementary strengths, drawing upon the different perspectives from within the team to solve problems, and reinforcing the value of each team member in the process. This all creates positive loops of collaboration. Instead of waiting around to solve problems or trying to go solo, people work together naturally, drawing out assets from each other and allowing the whole team to move faster with agility.

CREATE PSYCHOLOGICAL SAFETY THROUGH VULNERABILITY

A few years ago, Google's "People Operations" department (what other organizations typically call Human Resources) decided to figure out what set apart the most effective teams within the company. The group embarked on an initiative called "Project Aristotle." Over two hundred interviews were conducted across 180 different teams. The researchers also created a survey to help assess team effectiveness. Gathering quantifiable data is important for just about everything Google does.

After two years of research, the Project Aristotle team uncovered five key dynamics that distinguished the most successful teams from the rest:[23]

- **Psychological Safety:** People feel safe to take risks and be vulnerable in front of each other.
- **Dependability:** People get things done on time with high quality.
- **Structure and Clarity:** Team members have clear roles, plans, and goals.
- **Meaning of Work:** The work is personally important to all team members.
- **Impact of Work:** People believe their work matters and creates positive change.

Google's researchers concluded that psychological safety is by far the most important piece of the puzzle. Without it, nothing else will dramatically move the performance needle. Psychological safety is something I've also seen as a critical success factor (in my work, I've sometimes referred to it as having a "safe environment" or a "culture of trust"). The lack of it is something I've seen stifle teams and entire organizations. When it exists, however, it enhances the other success factors highlighted in Google's findings, bringing intentions to life and driving successes that shine.

Google conducted its research to figure out the "formula" for successful teams. Because Google quantifies just about everything it does, the People Operations group wanted to deliver a recipe that anyone could use to build and lead a high-performing team. Charles

Duhigg's article about Google's findings in the *New York Times Magazine*[24] highlighted the challenge with Google's objective while recognizing the role of experience as the essential component of building psychological safety: "Project Aristotle is a reminder that when companies try to optimize everything, it's sometimes easy to forget that success is often built on experiences—like emotional interactions and complicated conversations and discussions of who we want to be and how our teammates make us feel—that can't really be optimized," he noted.

The soft stuff, the success factors that underlie a team's ultimate potential, is the hardest stuff to optimize. That's why it's impossible to fully mechanize the process of creating great teams. On the other hand, specific experiences *can* be optimized—like by stacking a team with diverse experiences through hiring or by simply helping everyone see the unique experiences and related assets that exist within the team. Consciously creating shared experiences with an opportunity to experience vulnerability can also help a team develop its XQ while building greater psychological safety.

Vulnerability, the most effective way to build psychological safety, isn't just a behavioral act performed by a person or team. It's a mindset that's part of a person's or team's XQ. Vulnerability is inherently risky. That's the nature of vulnerability: we might be judged for sharing our thoughts and feelings. But if you possess a mindset anchored in the belief that "self-disclosure leads to better and more productive relationships" or that "I'm comfortable sharing my thoughts and feelings, and how others respond says something about themselves but doesn't have to negatively impact me," you're better able to take a leap and be vulnerable. When these types of attitudes and beliefs are held by your entire team, the result is positive relationship loops. People will work together in ways that draw out the best in others. Vulnerability becomes a strategic tool for high performance.

Historically, however, there's been a social stigma tied to sharing personal struggles, whether past or present. I was raised at a time when showing emotion signified weakness, especially for boys and men. Because of my unusual and difficult home life, I never spoke about my family. I feared that people would judge me because of my mother's struggles. I feared judgment because I feared losing emotional connection with others, something I longed for because of my parents' limited availability as I was growing up. After I began sharing my story about my childhood and how I ended up caring for my mother toward the end of her life, however, I experienced the exact opposite of what I was fearful of: people actually moved toward me with empathy. That's the power of expressing vulnerability.

This is exactly what my group at HP did when we revolted against the traditional performance evaluation mandate. We didn't like the way it pigeonholed people into bell-curve distributions of performance, and we wanted to avoid such a restrictive process. We redefined the process into a model where everyone had an opportunity to understand, and then help, everyone else. Instead of having managers check off a series of boxes to provide a performance score for their team members, we used a more collaborative, qualitative 360-degree dialogue model. We created a repeatable process that delivered shared experiences for the entire team. The experiences were focused on appreciating people's strengths, identifying growth opportunities, and defining specific projects that could be used to advance the individual's and team's goals. We role-modeled vulnerability to set the stage for discussions about personal challenges and future growth opportunities. We took turns in the roles of facilitating the process, providing feedback, and being evaluated. We transformed the concept of "being evaluated" so that the process would be an opportunity to create connection rather than something everyone dreaded. People on our team no longer dreaded their year-end performance evaluations. We looked forward to the process because it brought us closer together and resulted in practical actions focused on making us better, both individually and as a team. The approach was so powerful that I developed a guide for it, which you can use with your own team to facilitate a similar process. I call it the XQ360 Process, and it's available for download as part of the Experiential Intelligence Toolkit at https://sorenkaplan .com/XQToolkit.

Get the XQ360 Process as Part of the XQ Toolkit

FOSTER ABILITIES AND KNOW-HOW

If psychological safety is the foundation of great teams, "dependability," along with "structure and clarity," are the means to get great things done. "Meaning of work" and "impact of work" provide purpose and motivation. Every team has the opportunity to develop itself to support Google's success factors as high-level abilities. Yet your team's abilities and know-how should also align with the type of work you do and what's needed for success in your industry. For example, teams in industries with rapidly changing market dynamics like technology or media often strive to become more "agile" to effectively function in today's disruptive environment. Agile teams possess mindsets focused on moving quickly and modifying project plans on a regular basis, often weekly or monthly. It's the exact opposite of how many teams in big companies set annual plans and stick to them no matter what. Agile teams go from sprint to sprint, challenging their mindsets and identifying the abilities and know-how necessary to achieve the goals of the following sprint. That is, before they complete a sprint, they've already started planning for the next one. Agility becomes a core ability of the team, supported by know-how in agile methodologies and tools.

There are a variety of ways you can support the development and amplification of your team's XQ, focused on growing and leveraging abilities and know-how:

- Use the XQ360 to replace or complement traditional performance evaluations.
- When running meetings, include a discussion of the success stories from the past month, quarter, or year to explore the mindsets, abilities, and know-how that contributed to those successes.
- Set up coaching groups between team members to move through the XQ development process, with a focus on surfacing the abilities and know-how most important for the future.
- Analyze your team's relationship loops, and work with your team to reshape them, using vulnerability as a strategic tool.

- Explore the relationship loops that exist between your team and other teams. Work with your team to reshape them in partnership with the other teams.

AMPLIFY XQ

Helping individuals develop their XQ grows the team's collective XQ. That's the dynamic involved in amplification. If you're leading a team, you have the opportunity to create a context for sharing and creating experiences that elevate each team member's game, as well as that of the entire team, producing a high-performing culture where everyone wins. But it has to start with you. It's one thing to ask others to step up and get vulnerable; it's another thing to role-model it so people can see how it's done.

Even if you're not a formal leader of a team, you can still serve as a role model. You don't even have to get vulnerable, if that's not your thing. Just talking about the experiences your team has had, the strengths that surfaced during those experiences, and how the overall team benefitted can start a positive relationship loop that amplifies everyone's individual XQ, as well as the team's.

I'll end this chapter with a few additional words about vulnerability because it can be such a success factor in developing individual and team XQ. Vulnerability begets vulnerability. When we open up and share stories, struggles, and emotions, we connect to other people as *people*. The book *Leadership and Self-Deception* highlights the importance of viewing people as *people* versus "objects." When team members view each other as objects, they see their peers as vehicles to use for personal gain, obstacles to blame, or irrelevancies that can be ignored. Vulnerability humanizes teams. Sharing personal experiences creates connections that enrich everyone. When we hear others' stories, we have an opportunity to connect our experience to theirs. We find common ground, often in the details of others' experiences. This is where Experiential Intelligence reinforces Emotional Intelligence, and vice versa.

Being vulnerable, showing empathy to others, and doing both in a consistent way over time shifts mindsets. By discussing your experiences working with people both inside and outside your organization, you can identify strengths and success factors that have served you well and that you want to leverage in the future. In order to do this, you may need to process difficult situations and emotions. That's normal.

You can carry your team through challenges and amplify its strengths with the power of positive emotions. Encouraging and energizing people through positive feelings like excitement, purpose, and contribution helps shift mindsets, develop abilities, and tap into the know-how of the team to achieve future goals.

CHAPTER TEN KEY MESSAGES:

- Teams are simply collections of people, each of whom carry their collective experiences, along with the impacts from those experiences and the mindsets, abilities, and know-how gained from them.
- Team XQ is the collective XQ of a team's individual members.

- Three design principles can help you tap into the complementary XQ that exists across team members while simultaneously amplifying your team's overall XQ:
  - Stack your team with diverse experiences
  - Foster positive relationship loops
  - Create psychological safety through vulnerability
- Simply discussing the experiences your team has had, the strengths that surfaced during those experiences, and how the overall team has benefitted from them can start a positive relationship loop that amplifies both individual XQ and team XQ.
- By developing your team's XQ, you can become a high-performing team that achieves goals, drives innovation, and responds to change and opportunities with greater agility.

11

ORGANIZATIONAL XQ

Chapter Eleven Video Overview

t's all connected.

Organizational XQ is the collection of complementary mind-sets, abilities, and know-how that drives strategy and business results. Discovering, amplifying, and leveraging Experiential Intelligence (XQ) across an organization involves using the approaches I describe in the Leadership XQ and Team XQ chapters to transform culture so you can better leverage your organization-wide XQ.

But there's a fundamental assumption that our society holds, and that most organizations blindly reinforce, that you must overcome to harness your organization's XQ. The assumption is this: *it's necessary to separate our inner personal lives from our work lives.*

It's common to conceal parts of ourselves and reveal just enough to save face, protect our egos, and build our personal brands. I did this for a long time myself. And it wasn't like doing so completely blocked my professional success; I still built a consulting business, traveled the world to speak to executives, and wrote articles and books. Yet as "successful" as I might have been on the outside, my compart-mentalization stifled my full potential. I see many leaders, managers, and employees experience this same dynamic. They're performing well, receiving accolades and bonuses—yet deep down they know they can do, and feel, better.

People's internal limitations surface no matter what they're doing or where. They can't always leave behind their unhelpful mindsets, for example, when they walk through the office—or home office—door. The impacts from people's experiences can either get in the way of daily performance or significantly limit their contributions at the highest level, or both. Until we recognize this human truth as something to strategically manage, individuals, teams, and organizations will never reach their full potential.

As I mentioned before, compart-mentalization isn't all dysfunctional. We need to manage our inner personal lives in relation to our professional pursuits to stay focused, not to mention remain socially appropriate based on the situation. But broader cultural forces in society and business keep the worlds of personal and professional disconnected, even stigmatizing people who show vulnerability at work. These headwinds can become a challenge to growing organizational XQ.

The first step in moving toward greater organizational XQ is to recognize the long-held assumption that people don't and shouldn't bring their full selves to the workplace. Everyone brings the whole of who they are with them, assets included, wherever they go. Some organizations leverage these assets better than others. The question is how to best tap into the mindsets, abilities, and know-how that inherently exist across people and teams in ways that amplify and grow the latent XQ that already exists within your organization.

EMBED XQ INTO YOUR ORGANIZATIONAL CULTURE

Organizational culture is created and reinforced every day through people's experiences. The things that happen within an organization shape people's mindsets about what is good, bad, effective, and rewarded. These attitudes and beliefs influence how people act. Their behavior creates more experiences because everyone is always taking cues from what everyone else says and does. These experiences cement prevailing attitudes and beliefs, which can become unquestioned assumptions about how to behave at work. These large-scale relationship loops can either lead to an organization becoming a great place to work, or to downward spirals of toxicity.

You may have heard that "culture eats strategy for breakfast," which basically means that culture is so powerful that it can stifle the best of business strategies if you don't take it into account. It probably seems obvious that toxic cultures aren't good for employee morale and get in the way of performance and results. Despite the general recognition that culture is a critical success factor in business, however, toxic organizational cultures can fly under the radar for a long time. These cultures are often exacerbated by a combination of formal and informal policies, procedures, rewards, and poor leadership behavior.

For example, during the early days of Uber, I used the service to order a ride from the Newark airport in New Jersey to New York City. When the driver pulled up, it was hard to tell it was my ride because there wasn't an Uber sign in the window of the car. The driver said he didn't display the sign because the airport police would give him a $1,000 fine if he got caught picking up passengers. "Why would you take that risk?" I asked. "Because if I get a ticket, I'll just send it into Uber, and they'll pay it!" he enthusiastically replied.

From the start, Uber had an aggressive approach to everything it did. Uber's employees were accused of submitting over five thousand fake ride requests to Lyft as an underhanded strategy to derail its competitor. Uber also threatened journalists that it would dig up and publicize personal dirt on anyone who criticized the company. And the company was caught in Portland using special technology to sidestep local transportation regulations. Following this controversy, twenty Uber employees were fired for maintaining a culture that accepted and even encouraged sexual harassment. Even with public backlash brewing due to media reports of Uber's toxic culture, one of the company's board members was forced to resign after making a sexist comment during a large employee meeting focused on addressing the rampant sexism at the company. Unbelievable, but true.

It's important to acknowledge that many books and articles, and society in general, talk about organizations as if they are people. In many ways, American corporations are treated and behave like citizens—they can donate to political causes or can be held liable for environmental mishaps (though, notably, corporations typically shield the human beings inside them from negative consequences). But a company is not a single person, even if the law gives corporations similar rights as those given to citizens. This fact is blindingly obvious, but it needs to be said. So, in the case of Uber, it wasn't some single corporate entity doing a whole host of improper things. It was its people. Not everyone, but enough in high places and across the company to instill a mindset with attitudes and beliefs that led to and allowed brazen behavior.

Organizations are simply groups of people who bring their own unique history of individual experiences, self-limiting beliefs, auto-pilot behaviors—and assets—to the physical and virtual office. Their interactions create experiences that lead to collective attitudes and beliefs—right or wrong—about which abilities and know-how are needed to achieve the goals of the business.

Opportunities for more explicitly embedding XQ into your organizational culture arise when you look at what's already working well and what strengths exist, rather than merely viewing what exists through a negative lens. Whereas many people tend to want to focus exclusively on what's broken, dysfunctional, and getting in the way, the goal is to flip that around. Ruminating on the negative stifles motivation and zaps energy. A positive focus inspires and mobilizes.

This isn't about ignoring the realities that exist in most organizations—that things can very well be broken and shouldn't be ignored, or else they'll continue to fester and crop up as even larger problems later. A fundamental premise of Experiential Intelligence, however, is that everyone possesses strengths. It's important to strike a delicate balance between seeing the positive and still acknowledging that, while everyone has assets to apply, their past experiences may have produced self-limiting beliefs and autopilot responses that could be obstacles to performance.

If you want to infuse greater XQ into your organization's culture, you can use four key strategies:

1. **Create new experiences** that reinforce new or existing mindsets, abilities, and know-how for individuals and teams.
2. **Develop people's abilities**, focusing specifically on what is needed to achieve your vision, mission, and strategy.
3. **Scale Experiential Intelligence** to spread the most powerful existing mindsets, abilities, and know-how throughout the organization.
4. **Foster positive relationship loops** that amplify XQ and accelerate collaboration, innovation, and performance.

Applying these strategies provides a structure for uncovering and channeling people's individual and shared experiences to fully leverage everyone's mindsets, abilities, and know-how—your organizational XQ.

1. CREATE NEW EXPERIENCES

Create experiences that reinforce positive mindsets focused on innovation, collaboration, excellent service, sustainability, and anything else important for the future. For example, sharing stories during meetings about how certain people and teams achieved great things, went above and beyond to solve a customer problem, or worked together in new and innovative ways, conveys what's valued and why. Providing people with formal and informal rewards and recognition reinforces the mindsets, abilities, and know-how valued by the organization.

There's nothing worse for an organization's culture than asking people for ideas and then doing nothing with them. I've seen this over and over again when leadership asks for suggestions, innovations, and ideas but doesn't really want to do or change anything once they get them. One large insurance company I worked with wanted to shift their culture to promote innovation. The insurance industry by its very nature is risk averse. Their CEO, however, was committed to doing whatever it would take to create a culture of innovation. That's why she sponsored an experiential training program for all 3,800 team members in the company. The training wasn't traditional. It delivered a hands-on experience with "design thinking" that helped people identify challenges, generate and prioritize solutions, and create prototypes of the best ideas—all in a four-hour session. But it didn't end there. Every manager was asked to send their top opportunities to the executive team and then report out several months later what they had done to implement the best ones. The approach created a shared experience of tapping into the organization's collective wisdom to create ideas. More importantly, it led to sharing, recognizing, and celebrating ideas that had actually been implemented. The whole experience wasn't just a rah-rah, feel-good event. It delivered real value. Experiences communicate what's important to the organization, which shape mindsets so that you get more of what's most valued.

2. DEVELOP ABILITIES

To effectively compete, organizations need the right talent who can define compelling strategies and get things done. According to the World Economic Forum's *The Future of Jobs Report* in 2020,[25] the top skills for the future of work include:

- Analytical thinking and innovation
- Active learning and learning strategies
- Complex problem-solving
- Critical thinking and analysis
- Creativity, originality, and initiative
- Leadership and social influence
- Technology use, monitoring, and control
- Technology design and programming
- Resilience, stress tolerance, and flexibility
- Reasoning, problem-solving and ideation
- Emotional Intelligence (EQ)
- Troubleshooting and user experience
- Service orientation
- Systems analysis and evaluation
- Persuasion and negotiation

In the context of Experiential Intelligence, what the World Economic Forum labels as skills are primarily mindsets and abilities. That's why their report recognizes that "when it comes to employers providing workers with training opportunities for reskilling and upskilling, in contrast to previous years, employers are expecting to lean more fully on informal as opposed to formal learning ... [and that] 94 percent of business leaders report that they expect employees to pick up new skills on the job ... using both formal and informal methods of skills acquisition."

While some of these skills, like "technology use, monitoring, and control," could be learned through formal education and training courses, most of the others are less about "skills" and more about abilities. Abilities aren't necessarily taught to people through books or online courses. Developing "leadership and social influence," for example, often requires years of experience working with people and teams. "Resilience, stress tolerance, and flexibility" is usually developed over time through dealing with complex, challenging situations.

People notice what's rewarded, as well as what's ignored. Seek out exemplary people who embody what you want more of and publicly recognize them for their small, medium, and large contributions and achievements. When you do, highlight exactly the abilities you're recognizing and why so that everyone understands what competencies are most important for the future. Doing this generates an awareness of what's valued that becomes the foundation and motivating force for both formal and informal personal and professional development.

Of course, you first need to identify the abilities that will be most important for your organization in the future. Then, use various programs, like employee onboarding, leadership development, and rewards and recognition, to instill these. It's not just about telling people what abilities are needed for success. Give them the opportunity to understand and develop those abilities through practice.

3. SCALE EXPERIENTIAL INTELLIGENCE

When workers who possess significant knowledge about customers, business processes, or anything else important end up retiring or leaving a company, it can be a problematic brain drain for the organization. It's already hard to find good talent, so when someone who possesses deep knowledge about the organization leaves, it's a big loss. Organizations of the future need to tap into people's XQ through intentionally capturing and sharing the most strategic and useful mindsets, abilities, and know-how.

Understanding the value of tapping into and leveraging the vast experience that exists within organizations was exactly what led me to found Praxie. Organizations today need to move quickly, remain agile, and innovate in everything they do. The only way to do that is to fully take advantage of all of the formal and informal assets that exist across their people and teams. It's all about "scaling" Experiential Intelligence by capturing and then making available the know-how, abilities, and even the mindsets that give you an edge. You can do this in many ways, from traditional training programs to using technology to digitize work processes. The goal is to provide expert resources that allow anyone to hit the ground running, stop reinventing the wheel, and build upon what already exists.

Those in positions to build XQ into business processes and create programs that diffuse XQ across the organization might consider doing so in the following ways:

- Provide development programs to help people become versed in how experience impacts personal and professional success

- Create mentoring programs to support and grow emerging leaders
- Create peer-to-peer coaching programs focused on growing EQ and XQ
- Design talent management and development that focus on mindsets, abilities, and know-how
- Design recruiting and hiring practices that focus on the mindsets, abilities, and know-how needed for the future
- Design performance management systems to include collaborative development sessions that focus on recognizing mindsets, abilities, and know-how and identifying growth opportunities that can be supported within current relationship loops
- Create "best practices" that codify the mindsets, abilities, and know-how of those who do things best; develop tools, templates, and processes that give others a process for doing what has led to prior success

Whatever programs you use, the ideal approach amplifies the existing mindsets, abilities, and know-how in the organization that will make the biggest difference in shaping your future.

4. FOSTER POSITIVE RELATIONSHIP LOOPS

Positive relationship loops are at the heart of high-performing organizational cultures. As explained earlier, positive loops are "generative"

181

because the players in the relationship loop amplify each other's unique strengths, elevating everyone's game. Those within this kind of relationship usually have some awareness that they're in a positive loop, even if they don't use that language specifically. They appreciate and recognize that everyone in the relationship brings unique attributes to the table that inspire bigger and better things in everyone else. The relationship often holds a higher purpose that goes beyond the individual by focusing on aspirational benefits for the customer, team, organization, or community.

The most effective organizational cultures are founded upon positive mindsets that encourage people to contribute their unique assets to this kind of shared purpose. When people successfully collaborate, they demonstrate what's possible, creating learning experiences for those who witness their results. These collective experiences in turn reinforce the belief that "anything's possible," which inspires corresponding behavior: actions focused on breaking through to the next level. It's a cycle that solidifies the norms and values of organizational culture.

Anyone can help reinvent the culture of their organization by role-modeling XQ, which is essentially the process of amplification that I've previously described. The challenge is that many corporate cultures put people in an impossible double-bind situation—they're encouraged to be vulnerable during team-building sessions and in performance reviews, yet they're often judged for doing so. It's tough to embrace approaches that apply the principles of positive psychology when we're pulled down by negative relationship loops that pervade everyday experiences.

That being said, because humility and vulnerability are the contagious starting points for tapping into XQ, demonstrating it through personal disclosure can help others tap into the power of XQ themselves. From this standpoint, we all have the ability to proactively shape organizational culture.

MAKE XQ A BUSINESS IMPERATIVE

Building XQ into your organizational culture isn't just about getting greater employee engagement. It's also about creating competitive advantage and driving innovation. It's also not about conducting a one-time event, like a training session. Embedding XQ into your culture to yield greater organizational XQ should ideally involve a multipronged approach. In addition to the strategies in this chapter, you might also need to look at functional areas specific to your own organization. For example, most organizations recruit, hire, and develop people using targeted job descriptions anchored in specific skillsets. Organizations that approach hiring and developing people this way miss huge untapped reservoirs of talent, new ideas, and opportunities. Building XQ into the culture of your organization might involve updating the processes involved in identifying, recruiting, and screening candidates so that you can tap into the mindsets, abilities, and know-how that aren't constrained by keywords in a job description.

Your organization delivers experiences to people every day. How you treat employees and customers, how you compete in the market, and how you engage with vendors and partners all create experiences for people inside and outside your organization. These are the relationship loops that continually reinforce the underlying attitudes and beliefs of your culture. They're also the relationship loops in which people can apply their XQ to achieve your business goals. You can leave it up to chance. Or you can design experiences that amplify specific mindsets, abilities, and know-how across people and teams. When you embed XQ into your culture, you grow your organizational XQ.

CHAPTER ELEVEN KEY MESSAGES:

- Organizational XQ is the collection of complementary mindsets, abilities, and know-how that drives strategy and business results

- Society and most organizations blindly reinforce the assumption that it's necessary to separate our inner personal lives from our work lives.

- An opportunity exists to replace the long-held assumption that people shouldn't bring their full selves to the workplace with a new focus on tapping into the mindsets, abilities, and know-how across people and teams to amplify and grow the latent XQ that already exists within organizations.

- Organizational culture is created and reinforced every day by shaping people's mindsets through experiences that communicate what is good, bad, effective, and rewarded.

- Building Experiential Intelligence into organizational culture involves creating positive experiences that reinforce the mindsets and behavior needed for the future, which can be done using four strategies:

- Create new experiences
- Develop people's abilities
- Scale Experiential Intelligence
- Foster positive relationship loops
- When you embed XQ into your culture, you grow your organizational XQ, which can then transform the culture and deliver breakthroughs in innovation and business performance.

12

COMMUNITY XQ

Chapter Twelve Video Overview

One night, a few years before the pandemic, I was sitting around the table with a group of friends, and the topic of race came up. I asked my friend Karl, who's Black, if he or his family had experienced racism in our suburb, Walnut Creek, just east of San Francisco.

Karl is originally from South Central Los Angeles. He knows all too well the challenges of growing up in a tough environment. He has "made it" by many of today's standards. He attended college and then earned an MBA. At the time of our dinner together, he was working in IT at Chevron. He is married and has two children who attend local Walnut Creek public schools, some of the top ones in California.

After I asked the question, Karl responded with his own question.

"Do you know how many times I was pulled over by the Walnut Creek police for no apparent reason last year?"

"No idea," I replied.

"Six," Karl stoically said.

"Six?!" our group exclaimed.

"That's right. I'm always very polite, keep both hands on the wheel, don't reach for anything anywhere in the car unless asked to do so, and reply with 'sir' or 'ma'am' when I'm spoken to."

The rest of us, three other couples, were speechless. None of us could believe that Karl—one of the nicest people we knew—could experience this type of thing in our own backyard. Our stunned silence signaled we wanted to better understand his experience.

He continued. "One of those times, I was driving home, passing through downtown. The officer asked where I was coming from. I told him, 'From work.' He asked where I worked, and I said at Chevron. He then asked me, 'At what station?'"

"'At what station'?!" all of us gasped. The police officer assumed that Karl worked at one of our local gas stations rather than considering the possibility he might have a position at the company's corporate office.

"Another time, a female police officer pulled me over. As she approached my window, I saw her put her hand on her gun. Her whole body was shaking. I don't know which of us was more scared, she or me."

We collectively expressed our surprise, anger, and sadness that our friend had these types of experiences on a consistent basis, just down the street from where we were all sitting together. The town that we believed was a welcoming place to live wasn't welcoming to Karl.

I asked him how these experiences had affected him and his family. "Well, I'm going to be giving 'the talk' to my fourteen-year-old son really soon," he said.

"The talk?" I asked, knowing that "the talk" in my house meant a discussion about the birds and the bees.

"As a Black man, it's very important to understand what to do and what not to do when you're pulled over by the police. I need to teach my son how to stay safe," explained Karl.

I thought about my own experience with the Walnut Creek police. I had been pulled over once twenty years prior for rolling through a stop sign. The officer gave me a ticket, and I went on my way. That was the extent of it. I never worried that I would be stopped for no apparent reason. I never thought about how to behave if I was pulled over. I never feared for my daughters' safety if they were stopped when driving downtown.

The discussion with Karl was a poignant one for me. I felt surprised, angry, and ashamed that my friend had so many examples to share of being stopped by the police. I felt sad that he was compelled to educate his son about how to stay safe throughout what he viewed would be a lifelong series of inevitable unwarranted interactions with the police. While I was coaching my daughter's soccer team, he was coaching his son on how to survive as a Black male in our community.

In retrospect, it's obvious that Karl could easily possess a different experience than me, even living in the same town. We indeed shared experiences related to activities at our kids' school, social gatherings like the barbeque at my house, and other local events. Yet, Karl possessed a vastly different experience when it came to navigating life in our town because of his skin color. I have since heard other Black men share similar stories, including the need for "the talk" with their sons.

SHARED EXPERIENCES CREATE CONNECTION

Shared experiences bring people together. Bonds are created when people experience things at the same time and in the same place, whether on a sports team, at school, in war, in an organization, at church, in a community, or in a family. Even when our experiences occur at different times and places, they can still serve to create connections. When we discover that we have had a similar experience as someone at a dinner party, through a spontaneous discussion with a stranger in a restaurant, or in a business meeting, positive rapport often results. We see the other as relatable.

Communities of Shared Experience (CoSEs) are just that: they're groups of people who have experienced something similar in life. Being part of a CoSE doesn't mean you have to have had the same experience at the same time with someone, nor share every experience with everyone else in the group. Rather, it means that you have had similar life experiences as others and can relate to the types of circumstances and feelings tied to those experiences. It can also mean you share specific mindsets, abilities, and know-how that are tied to those experiences.

Most of us belong to multiple CoSEs. In my case, I grew up with a mother with schizophrenia, so I'm part of a community with other people who have parents with mental illness. Both my parents are Caucasian, so I'm part of a CoSE with other white men. My parents were also in a group of about four hundred "Sufis" when I was growing up, so I share experiences with people who grew up in alternative spiritual communities. I went to one of the top public high schools in

California, which helped prepare me to attend some of the top universities in California, so I'm part of a CoSE with people who have had the privilege of quality higher education. When I moved to Silicon Valley after school, I became part of a CoSE with people involved in entrepreneurial business ventures.

When I've shared with others that I've had a parent with mental illness, that singular experience becomes the bonding focus. Differences in life circumstances or skin color aren't necessarily in the foreground when emotionally connecting with another person around deep, shared feelings, like the feelings of uncertainty and fear involved with having a parent who is utterly unpredictable. Or the disappointment involved with not receiving caring parenting as a child. Or being overwhelmed in taking on responsibility for your struggling parent, who rejects your care because they see it as unwanted control. Shared experiences create the opportunity for shared empathy. You feel what they feel. They feel what you feel.

Even when you share common experiences with someone in your CoSE, they may still have vastly different experiences from you in other areas of life. The immensely diverse array of our experiences is what makes us all unique. Take the fact that both Karl and I live in the same geographic area of Walnut Creek. We share the same geographic, community-based experiences. But Karl is also part of a CoSE with other Black men. As a white male, I don't share that experience, which probably accounts for why I've never been pulled over by the Walnut Creek police for no reason. For many Black parents, there's a concrete reason why "the talk" is a term that's well understood and passed down generation after generation. Within the CoSE I share with other white men, that version of "the talk" is hardly on our radar.

There are many different CoSEs you may belong to. Some were thrust upon you as a child without your choosing—like the composition of your family, the different childhood challenges you may have experienced, the color of your skin, your socioeconomic status, and countless other factors. When it comes to understanding yourself, as well as others, it can be helpful to identify the CoSEs that you belong to. Here are some spheres in which people share experiences and form bonds:

- Art
- Education
- Ethnicity
- Family structure
- Gender identity
- Generational identity
- Hobbies
- Job roles
- Language
- Mental health
- Neighborhoods
- Organizations
- Physical health
- Race
- Recreation
- Religion
- Sexual orientation
- Social causes
- Socioeconomic status
- Spirituality

- Sports
- Trauma

What's also noteworthy is that unless you have had experiences associated with a specific CoSE, you may not feel like a part of that community, even if you share certain attributes with those who affiliate with it. For example, my father's side of the family is Jewish. My grandparents fled France and came to New York City just before World War II and the German invasion of their country. My father grew up going to Hebrew school and synagogue, had a bar mitzvah when he turned thirteen, and celebrated Passover and other Jewish holidays. My mother, on the other hand, grew up in a Methodist family, and her father was a minister and missionary. After I was born, however, my parents moved us to California to join a Sufi spiritual community. The only time I was exposed to Jewish traditions growing up was when I would visit my relatives back in New York during my school break, which would coincide with Passover.

I never internalized "feeling Jewish" as a child, even though I gained some knowledge of Jewish traditions. During college, however, I had an experience that shifted my sense of identity. I met a neighbor in my apartment building who, hearing my last name, asked me if I was Jewish. "Kaplan" is a common last name among Ashkenazi Jews. Without really thinking about it or providing any sort of explanation, I told him I wasn't. But after a brief discussion about my family's history fleeing Europe, as well as the fact that my great-great uncle, Jacob Kaplan, had served as the Chief Rabbi in France, my neighbor bluntly responded, "If you were living in Europe during World War II and captured by the Nazis, you would have been sent to the gas chamber."

He was right. At the same time, though, I didn't *feel* Jewish. I didn't understand most of the deeper meanings behind the traditions and holidays. I had never been to Israel. I didn't practice Judaism. This experience stuck with me and later inspired me to understand more about my heritage. In the following years, I would learn more about my family's history during the occupation of France, meet my Jewish relatives who had remained in France, and visit the infamous concentration camp Dachau. Through these experiences that exposed me to new knowledge, relationships, and opportunities for empathy, I gained a greater sense of affiliation with my Jewish CoSE.

FIND STRENGTHS IN YOUR COMMUNITIES OF SHARED EXPERIENCE

Within a Community of Shared Experience exists a wide range of historical experiences. Some experiences may have caused multigenerational trauma and persistent social challenges over time. Other experiences might have instilled a set of strengths within the community that allows it to thrive. Or, sometimes both are the case. The question, and opportunity, is how to recognize a community's challenges and obstacles to overcome while concurrently celebrating and leveraging the unique strengths—the mindsets, abilities, and know-how—that the community can use to foster positive social change.

Consider your own CoSEs. What communities are you part of? How many do you have?

Imagine a multidimensional Venn diagram in which your CoSEs intersect. You might have three, four, or twelve communities overlapping; it's up to you to decide how many CoSEs you feel connected to. Regardless of how many you resonate with, they've all most likely contributed to your mindsets and how you view the world in some way. They've provided the context for the things you've done that helped you develop specific abilities and know-how. The combination of your CoSEs and the experiences you've had within them are unique to you.

If you want to understand your CoSEs better, make your own multidimensional Venn diagram. Use as many intersecting circles as communities you have. Label the circles with the names of your CoSEs.

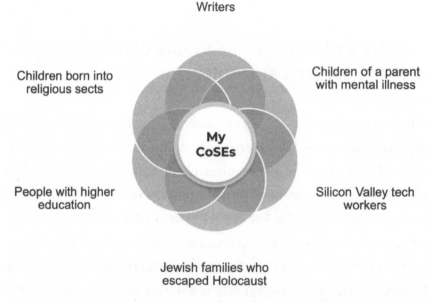

Writers

Children born into religious sects

Children of a parent with mental illness

My CoSEs

People with higher education

Silicon Valley tech workers

Jewish families who escaped Holocaust

Communities of Shared Experience Venn Diagram Template
Identify Your Communities of Shared Experience

A simple template can help you identify your CoSEs and how they have contributed to your Experiential Intelligence (XQ). List your communities and how they've led to your strengths. Try to put a positive spin on what you've gained from your experiences, even if your experiences have been difficult at times. For example, even though I'm part of a CoSE with others who have a parent with mental illness, I learned to appreciate small moments of connection with my mother, and I obtained a high degree of self-sufficiency from needing to fend for myself growing up. The template below describes my own CoSEs and what I've gained from them.

My Communities	My Related Strengths
What Communities of Shared Experience (CoSEs) have the experiences in your life led you to be part of, either by circumstance or by conscious choice?	What strengths did you develop due to your experiences in the Community of Shared Experience? What mindsets (beliefs and assumptions), abilities (attributes and insights), and know-how (knowledge and skills) did you obtain from your experiences that can be used to help you achieve your goals in the future?
1 Children of a parent with mental illness	Ability to appreciate small positive attributes in others
2 Children born into religious sects	Belief that I am autonomous and can create my own path in life
3 Jewish families who escaped Holocaust	Desire to make the world a better, more empathetic place
4 People with higher education	Ability to analyze and understand abstract ideas
5 Silicon Valley tech workers	Mindset that embraces risk-taking and innovation
6 Writers	Ability to use simple language to communicate complex ideas

CoSE Strengths Template
Identify the Strengths Gained from Your Communities

Now, consider other people you know, whether your family, friends, or team at work. If you have the opportunity, compare your multidimensional Venn diagrams and discuss:

- How many intersecting circles do each of you have?
- What CoSEs do you have in common?
- Which CoSEs are different?

- What strengths did each of you gain from the experiences you have had in your CoSEs?
- In what ways can you share your strengths with each other to have a positive impact in your lives?

Connecting with a CoSE outside your own occurs through empathy, which provides an opportunity to gain a deeper understanding of the community and share in the collective strengths of its members. While each CoSE has its unique characteristics, there are still many related experiences we all share as human beings, like the search for meaning, the desire to feel significance, and the need for human connection and love.

CHAPTER TWELVE KEY MESSAGES:

- When people have shared experiences, they often form emotional connections anchored by a common identity.
- Communities of Shared Experience (CoSEs) are groups of people who have experienced something similar in life, which results in mutual mindsets, abilities, and know-how.
- Everyone belongs to various CoSEs, some which are based on life circumstances and some of which are chosen.
- An opportunity exists to recognize a community's challenges and obstacles to overcome while concurrently celebrating and leveraging the unique strengths—the mindsets, abilities, and know-how—that the community can use to foster positive social change.

13

BRING IT HOME

Chapter Thirteen Video Overview

Experiential Intelligence (XQ) is an intuitive concept that's long overdue as a mainstream idea. Few theories of intelligence address the deeper dynamics involved in what makes us tick. They strive to generalize and, in so doing, overlook how our unique experiences and assets contribute to achieving our own relative definitions of success.

We are all much more than our scores: IQ, SAT, ACT, and GMAT scores; performance evaluations; and bank account balances. I wrote this book because we need a better way to describe what makes each and every one of us uniquely ourselves, and to challenge society's pull to quantify our inherent worth using numbers and bell curves. When you look at yourself, your team, your organization, or your communities as merely a set of numbers, you become numb to what makes you, you—and what you have to offer the world.

If you took the opportunity to dive deeper into developing your XQ using the tools in this book, you probably realize that Experiential Intelligence isn't just for business. XQ is clearly useful in that context, but XQ is equally applicable to personal relationships, families, schools, and other areas. That's because, whatever social context we might find ourselves in, we're all just people coming together with human needs and emotions, trying to make sense of ourselves, others, and life. We're all shaped by our circumstances, carry the impacts of our experiences, and use the assets that we've gained over time as we move forward to navigate the world. And, while XQ can certainly help you understand yourself better, it can also be used to proactively design programs that facilitate advancements in education, psychology, parenting, group processes, and more.

XQ has existed since humans first walked the earth. As social creatures, we take on attitudes and beliefs aligned to the environment and culture in which we live. We gain "street smarts," no matter where our street is located, so we can operate as effectively as possible in the world. Sometimes the smarts we develop through our experiences help us, and sometimes they outsmart us later in life because, while they were once useful, they eventually end up undermining our success.

I've shared my own journey with Experiential Intelligence to bring the concept to life in a practical way that models the type of thinking, feeling, and sharing that's important for developing XQ. The stories that I've shared are indeed unique to me, but the process of leveraging the mindsets, abilities, and know-how gained from experiences—whether positive or negative—to achieve breakthroughs both personally and in business is available to anyone.

When we understand the past by embracing a "both/and" view, we're better able to achieve our goals. It can be difficult to let go of a purely negative—or positive—perspective of an experience, person, or idea. Connecting to the emotions of *both* joy *and* sorrow when reflecting on an experience, for example, isn't easy, even when those two emotions coexist. Holding the good and the bad, the positive and the negative, the painful and the joyous together, however, builds XQ.

Embracing competing and potentially paradoxical ideas about what happened to you, what the impacts were, and how you feel about them is part of both Emotional Intelligence (EQ) and Experiential Intelligence. For instance, my mother's passing left me to reflect on my experience of having a parent with mental illness. On the one hand, she met very few of my needs throughout my life. On the other hand, she had imparted countless positive impacts through her little quips of wisdom and in the moments we'd shared—most of which I could only see after she was gone. Eventually, I was able to concurrently hold that my mother was an inadequate parent while still having an appreciation for what she was able to provide, given her circumstances. As my viewpoint expanded to hold these positive and negative impacts together, I also began to recognize my father's contributions to my strengths in new ways. His monumental commitment to his spiritual community, along with his powerful work ethic driven by a higher purpose, set an example for me to find meaning in and be dedicated to whatever I do. As much as I was negatively impacted by my family's dynamics growing up, I also received incredible assets from them that I use today.

My mother was a prolific writer, having authored several hundred poems, and she used creative metaphors to describe her experience of the world. In the last few years of her life, she shared two profound thoughts with me. First, she said, "If you want something but can't have it, you just change what you want." She had learned this lesson over her many years of being dependent on others and unable to apply her own intelligence to achieve tangible things in the world. She embraced this belief to live the best life possible and to find emotional peace amid her challenging circumstances.

Later, she shared the second nugget of wisdom, saying, "If you love, you learn to listen." Her truth applies to both ourselves and to other people. If you love yourself, you're able to listen to your own thoughts and feelings with empathy and without judgment. As a result, you start to gain a better picture of who you are, as perfectly imperfect as you may be. By accepting yourself, you gain the mindset and ability to grow both your EQ and your XQ. And when you listen to others, you become better able to empathically understand who they are as well, as imperfect as they, too, may be. It's through listening, and love, that we learn to see, accept, and help ourselves—and others.

The quest to grow XQ is the quest to know yourself at a more deeply meaningful level. When you know yourself, you become more present in everyday life. You recognize that inherent strengths exist within everyone, even when those assets aren't immediately transparent. When you view XQ as real intelligence, you see that we all possess the capacity to discover new possibilities within ourselves and in the world.

Douglas Adams, author of *The Hitchhiker's Guide to the Galaxy*, once wrote, "I may not have gone where I intended to go, but I think

I have ended up where I needed to be."[26] We all make meaning for ourselves. When we're consumed by self-limiting beliefs, it's easy to think we're broken or relegated to unfortunate circumstances. The journey to greater XQ is the process of figuring out what works and what doesn't today, so that you can change your circumstances to create a better tomorrow.

Acknowledgments

L ife is a scrapbook of experiences, most of which include other people. I couldn't have written this book without the contributions of many others who, both knowingly and unwittingly, have helped write my book.

A big thanks to John Willig, my agent, who, based on his decades of experience in the publishing industry, saw the potential of *Experiential Intelligence*. Matt Holt and the team at BenBella have played a significant role in making this book a reality. Their ability to transform my ideas into a tangible book for others to experience embodies their higher purpose. I also give a joyful nod to Jen Singer, who used her ability as a motivational sounding board to help catalyze my early thoughts into the seeds that blossomed into this book.

Marty and his community of like-hearted "rascals," Ben, John, Jonathan, Matt, and Rob, have become friends and confidants as we buck the stereotype of what it means to be male in our culture. By practicing vulnerability and nonjudgmental attunement in the spirit of seeking equanimity, I have learned much from this group of amazing men, which is reflected throughout the pages of this book.

My colleagues and coaches, Sheri Wong, John Schinnerer, Sara Truebridge, Kristin Bodiford, Piri Ackerman-Barger, and Lindsey Godwin, each contributed in their own special way to my understanding of myself, my role in the world, and the experience I could deliver to others through this book. For those contributions, I thank you all.

So many others have been mentors in life, whether they know it or not: Jacques Kaplan, Claude Puiforcat Kaplan, John English, Roderick Dail, Hilda Dail, Rick Dail, Violaine Bachelier, Laurence Kaplan, Michael Howard, Mimi Howard, Monika Kohoviec, Terry Hogan, Frank Waltjen, Roy Jacques, Tom Taveggia, Dan Omans, Anna Seno, Bob Krinsky, Gayle Jay, Shari Duron, Stu Winby, Peter Gaarn, Peter Bartlett, Jenny Brandemuehl, Sheryl Root, Chris Fritz, Deb Colden, Sally Crawford, Janet Jones, Derrick Palmer, Cheryl Perkins, Diane Nijs, Liliya Terzieva, Celiane Camargo-Borges, Jeannette de Noord, David Yudis, Lacey Leone McLaughlin, Renee Dineen, Maureen Thompson, Debbie Hatmaker, Loressa Cole, Jean-Marc Pardonge, Gael Touya, Rebecca Romano, Carol Wittington, Brittany Simpson, Shaneen Wickenhauser, Jason Dinger, Stephanie Duggan, Pat Verduin, Santhi Ramesh, Shane Bertsch, Michael Olmstead, Lynne Lemberg, David Underwood, Jamie Donohoe, Bill Keene, Glenn Allen, Neal Maillet, Liisa Välikangas, Gary Hamel, and David Cooperrider.

To my friends and colleagues at Praxie—Lynch, Rothrock, Gabo, Eyal, McVal, Tatiana, Leslie, and Siarhei and team—you have continually inspired and pushed me to tap into and develop new assets every day. And, of course, there's Karen, whose fearlessness in tackling everyday strategic and tactical challenges has become a success factor in much of what I do.

I couldn't have written this book without the contributions of my immediate family. My mother, Jan, contributed her gift of love, wit, and acceptance. My father, Pascal, contributed the gift of higher purpose and wholehearted commitment. And my stepmother, Lynn, helped reveal to me the experience of being mothered, for which I will be forever grateful. My sister Teresa and I share some extraordinary experiences. Witnessing and learning from Teresa's resilience and wisdom has been inspiring beyond words. My sister Erin embodies deep humility, lightheartedness, a sense of adventure, and vulnerability, which I have seen transform relationships. My daughter Raelyn has role-modeled what it means to grow Experiential Intelligence, including the incredible self-awareness and amazing abilities that follow. My daughter Nola continually demonstrates how creating new experiences is entirely within our control, and when we do so with flair, we grow into who we need to be. My wife, Holli, is a life partner, thought partner, business partner, and partner in all our shared experiences. Our journey together has always been in exactly the direction we needed to take, even though at times we've lost sight of the path due to the fog. Fortunately, we were always there together, experiencing what we needed to individually so that we could come back together as stronger partners on the road to new experiences.

Notes

1. Alia Crum, "Does the Mind Impact Health? A Researcher's Insights," *Culture of Health Blog, Robert Wood Johnson Foundation*, October 12, 2017, https://www.rwjf.org/en/blog/2017/10/does-the-mind-impact-health.html.
2. Robert G. Kraft, "Bike Riding and the Art of Learning," *Change* 10, no. 6 (1978): 36, 40–42.
3. James T. Lamiell, *William Stern (1871–1938): A Brief Introduction to His Life and Works* (Lengerich, Germany: Pabst Science Publishers, 2010), 172.
4. Raymond B. Cattell, "Theory of Fluid and Crystallized Intelligence: A Critical Experiment," *Journal of Educational Psychology* 54, no. 1 (1963): 1–22, doi:10.1037/h0046743.
5. Daniel Goleman, *Emotional Intelligence: Why It Can Matter More Than IQ* (New York: Bantam Books, 1995).
6. Robert J. Sternberg, *Beyond IQ: A Triarchic Theory of Human Intelligence* (Cambridge: Cambridge University Press, 1985).
7. Howard Gardner, *Frames of Mind: The Theory of Multiple Intelligences* (New York: Basic Books, 1983).
8. Carol S. Dweck, *Mindset: The New Psychology of Success* (New York: Ballantine Books, 2016).
9. Jakob Pietschnig and Martin Voracek, "One Century of Global IQ Gains: A Formal Meta-Analysis of the Flynn Effect (1909–2013)," *Perspectives on Psychological Science* 10, no. 3 (2015): 282–306.

10. Bessel van der Kolk, *The Body Keeps the Score: Brain, Mind, and Body in the Healing of Trauma* (New York: Penguin Books, 2014).

11. Bruce D. Perry and Oprah Winfrey, *What Happened to You?: Conversations on Trauma, Resilience, and Healing* (New York: Flatiron Books, 2021).

12. Richard G. Tedeschi, Jane Shakespeare-Finch, Kanako Taku, and Lawrence G. Calhoun, *Posttraumatic Growth: Theory, Research, and Applications* (Abingdon, UK: Routledge, 2018).

13. Richard G. Tedeschi, "Growth After Trauma," *Harvard Business Review*, 2020, https://hbr.org/2020/07/growth-after-trauma.

14. Lorna Collier, "Growth After Trauma," *Monitor on Psychology* 47, no. 10 (November 2016), https://www.apa.org/monitor/2016/11/growth-trauma.

15. "Eye Movement Desensitization and Reprocessing (EMDR) Therapy," Clinical Practice Guideline for the Treatment of Posttraumatic Stress Disorder, American Psychological Association, last modified July 31, 2017, https://www.apa.org/ptsd-guideline/treatments/eye-movement-reprocessing.

16. D. O. Hebb, *The Organization of Behavior: A Neuropsychological Theory* (Hoboken, NJ: John Wiley & Sons, 1949).

17. Jeremy D. W. Clifton, Joshua D. Baker, Crystal L. Park, David B. Yaden, Alicia B. W. Clifton, Paolo Terni, Jessica L. Miller, Guang Zeng, Salvatore Giori, Andrew H. Schwartz et al., "Primal World Beliefs," *Psychological Assessment* 31, no. 1 (2019): 82–99, doi:10.1037/pas0000639.

18. Tedeschi, "Growth After Trauma."

19. The Arbinger Institute, *Leadership and Self-Deception: Getting Out of the Box* (Oakland, CA: Berrett-Koehler Publishers, Inc., 2018).

20. Brian O'Connell, "The C-Suite's Favorite Leadership Phrases—and How They Shaped Executives," The Society for Human Resource Management, September 8, 2021, https://www.shrm.org/resourcesandtools/hr-topics/people-managers/pages/wise-sayings-for-managers.aspx.

21. Gay Hendricks, *The Big Leap: Conquer Your Hidden Fear and Take Life to the Next Level* (New York: HarperOne, 2009).

22. Alison Reynolds and David Lewis, "Teams Solve Problems Faster When They're More Cognitively Diverse," *Harvard Business Review*, March 30, 2017, https://hbr.org/2017/03/teams-solve-problems-faster-when-theyre-more-cognitively-diverse.

23. "Guide: Understand Team Effectiveness," re:Work, Google, accessed February 10, 2022, https://rework.withgoogle.com/print/guides/5721312655835136/.

24. Charles Duhigg, "What Google Learned from Its Quest to Build the Perfect Team," *New York Times Magazine*, February 25, 2016, https://www.nytimes com/2016/02/28/magazine/what-google-learned-from-its-quest-to-build-the -perfect-team.html.

25. *The Future of Jobs Report 2020*, World Economic Forum, PDF file, https:// www3.weforum.org/docs/WEF_Future_of_Jobs_2020.pdf.

26. Douglas Adams, *The Long Dark Tea-Time of the Soul* (London: Pan Books, 1989).

Index

About the Author

S oren Kaplan is a bestselling and award-winning author and speaker, a columnist for *Inc. Magazine,* the founder of Praxie.com, and an affiliate at the Center for Effective Organizations at USC's Marshall School of Business. *Business Insider* and Thinkers50 have named him one of the world's top management experts and consultants.

Soren has advised, consulted to, and led professional development programs for thousands of executives at leading organizations around the world, including Disney, NBCUniversal, Kimberly-Clark, Colgate-Palmolive, Hershey, Red Bull, Medtronic, Roche, Philips, Cisco, Visa, JPMorgan Chase, Wells Fargo, Ascension Health, Kaiser Permanente, Star Alliance, CSAA Insurance Group, PwC, American Nurses Association, AARP, and many others. He has lectured at the University of Southern California's Marshall School of Business, the Copenhagen Business School, Melbourne Business School, Breda University of Applied Sciences in the Netherlands, and other MBA and executive education programs around the world.

Soren's debut book, *Leapfrogging*, was named "Best Leadership Book" by the Axiom Book Awards, and his book *The Invisible Advantage* received the "Best General Business Book" distinction by the International Book Awards. He has been quoted, published, and interviewed by Harvard Business Review, Fast Company, Forbes, CNBC, Vice, National Public Radio, the American Management Association, Strategy & Leadership, and the International Handbook on Innovation, among many others. He holds Masters and PhD degrees in organizational psychology.

Get the Experiential Intelligence Toolkit

Get the XQ Toolkit, a practical set of digital tools that you can use to develop your Experiential Intelligence and apply it to your team and organization.

- Group discussion guide
- Presentation templates
- Videos
- Interview guide
- 360 development process
- and more!

Visit **https://sorenkaplan.com** for details

Contact

Soren and his team are available for speaking, consulting, leadership development, and executive coaching. Visit www.sorenkaplan.com to learn more.